North Carolina Grade 8 Science

Dear Future Exam Success Story

First of all, **THANK YOU** for purchasing Mometrix study materials!

Second, congratulations! You are one of the few determined test-takers who are committed to doing whatever it takes to excel on your exam. **You have come to the right place.** We developed these study materials with one goal in mind: to deliver you the information you need in a format that's concise and easy to use.

In addition to optimizing your guide for the content of the test, we've outlined our recommended steps for breaking down the preparation process into small, attainable goals so you can make sure you stay on track.

We've also analyzed the entire test-taking process, identifying the most common pitfalls and showing how you can overcome them and be ready for any curveball the test throws you.

Standardized testing is one of the biggest obstacles on your road to success, which only increases the importance of doing well in the high-pressure, high-stakes environment of test day. Your results on this test could have a significant impact on your future, and this guide provides the information and practical advice to help you achieve your full potential on test day.

Your success is our success

We would love to hear from you! If you would like to share the story of your exam success or if you have any questions or comments in regard to our products, please contact us at **800-673-8175** or **support@mometrix.com**.

Thanks again for your business and we wish you continued success!

Sincerely,
The Mometrix Test Preparation Team

Written and edited by the Mometrix Test Preparation Team
Printed in the United States of America

TABLE OF CONTENTS

INTRODUCTION 1

STRATEGY #1 – PLAN BIG, STUDY SMALL 2

STRATEGY #2 – MAKE YOUR STUDYING COUNT 3

STRATEGY #3 – PRACTICE THE RIGHT WAY 4

STRATEGY #4 – PACE YOURSELF 6

TEST-TAKING STRATEGIES 7

PHYSICAL SCIENCE 11
- BASIC ORGANIZATION OF MATTER 11
- ATOM 11
- ATOMIC NUMBER AND MASS NUMBER 12
- EXAMPLE 13
- ELEMENTS, COMPOUNDS, SOLUTIONS, AND MIXTURES 13
- PERIODIC TABLE 14
- CHEMICAL FORMULAS 18
- PHYSICAL CHANGES 19
- CHEMICAL CHANGES 19
- CHEMICAL EQUATION 20
- LAW OF CONSERVATION OF MASS 20
- LAW OF CONSERVATION OF ENERGY 21
- EXAMPLE 21
- CONVERSION OF ENERGY WITHIN CHEMICAL SYSTEMS 22

LIFE SCIENCE 23
- POPULATIONS OF ANIMALS OR PLANTS 23
- ABIOTIC AND BIOTIC FACTORS 23
- SOURCES OF ENERGY IN ORGANISMS 23
- RELATIONSHIPS BETWEEN ORGANISMS 27
- COMPETITION 27
- ORGANISMS AND ENVIRONMENTAL CHANGES 28
- ECOLOGICAL SUCCESSION 30
- BIODIVERSITY 30
- ADAPTATION TO ENVIRONMENT 31
- NATURAL AND ARTIFICIAL SELECTION 31
- EVOLUTION 31
- EVIDENCE SUPPORTING EVOLUTION 32
- VIRUSES 36
- BACTERIA 36
- PROTISTS 36
- FUNGI 37
- EPIDEMIC AND PANDEMICS 37
- PLANTS 37

EARTH AND SPACE SCIENCE — 40
- PROPERTIES THAT CONTRIBUTE TO EARTH'S LIFE-SUSTAINING SYSTEM — 40
- HYDROSPHERE AND HYDROLOGIC CYCLE — 40
- ROCK CYCLE — 42
- LAYERS OF THE EARTH — 46
- NATURAL RESOURCES — 47
- LAYERS OF THE EARTH — 48
- PLATE TECTONICS — 48
- TYPES OF BIOMES — 53
- NATURAL RESOURCES — 54
- ENVIRONMENTAL IMPACTS — 55

PRACTICE TEST #1 — 60

ANSWER KEY AND EXPLANATIONS FOR TEST #1 — 73

PRACTICE TEST #2 — 80

ANSWER KEY AND EXPLANATIONS FOR TEST #2 — 94

HOW TO OVERCOME TEST ANXIETY — 101

ONLINE RESOURCES — 107

Introduction

Thank you for purchasing this resource! You have made the choice to prepare yourself for a test that could have a huge impact on your future, and this guide is designed to help you be fully ready for test day. Obviously, it's important to have a solid understanding of the test material, but you also need to be prepared for the unique environment and stressors of the test, so that you can perform to the best of your abilities.

For this purpose, the first section that appears in this guide is the **Success Strategies**. We've devoted countless hours to meticulously researching what works and what doesn't, and we've boiled down our findings to the most impactful steps you can take to improve your performance on the test. We start at the beginning with study planning and move through the preparation process, all the way to the testing strategies that will help you get the most out of what you know when you're finally sitting in front of the test.

We recommend that you start preparing for your test as far in advance as possible. However, if you've bought this guide as a last-minute study resource and only have a few days before your test, we recommend that you skip over the first two Success Strategies since they address a long-term study plan.

If you struggle with **test anxiety**, we strongly encourage you to check out our recommendations for how you can overcome it. Test anxiety is a formidable foe, but it can be beaten, and we want to make sure you have the tools you need to defeat it.

Strategy #1 – Plan Big, Study Small

There's a lot riding on your performance. If you want to ace this test, you're going to need to keep your skills sharp and the material fresh in your mind. You need a plan that lets you review everything you need to know while still fitting in your schedule. We'll break this strategy down into three categories.

Information Organization

Start with the information you already have: the official test outline. From this, you can make a complete list of all the concepts you need to cover before the test. Organize these concepts into groups that can be studied together, and create a list of any related vocabulary you need to learn so you can brush up on any difficult terms. You'll want to keep this vocabulary list handy once you actually start studying since you may need to add to it along the way.

Time Management

Once you have your set of study concepts, decide how to spread them out over the time you have left before the test. Break your study plan into small, clear goals so you have a manageable task for each day and know exactly what you're doing. Then just focus on one small step at a time. When you manage your time this way, you don't need to spend hours at a time studying. Studying a small block of content for a short period each day helps you retain information better and avoid stressing over how much you have left to do. You can relax knowing that you have a plan to cover everything in time. In order for this strategy to be effective though, you have to start studying early and stick to your schedule. Avoid the exhaustion and futility that comes from last-minute cramming!

Study Environment

The environment you study in has a big impact on your learning. Studying in a coffee shop, while probably more enjoyable, is not likely to be as fruitful as studying in a quiet room. It's important to keep distractions to a minimum. You're only planning to study for a short block of time, so make the most of it. Don't pause to check your phone or get up to find a snack. It's also important to **avoid multitasking**. Research has consistently shown that multitasking will make your studying dramatically less effective. Your study area should also be comfortable and well-lit so you don't have the distraction of straining your eyes or sitting on an uncomfortable chair.

The time of day you study is also important. You want to be rested and alert. Don't wait until just before bedtime. Study when you'll be most likely to comprehend and remember. Even better, if you know what time of day your test will be, set that time aside for study. That way your brain will be used to working on that subject at that specific time and you'll have a better chance of recalling information.

Finally, it can be helpful to team up with others who are studying for the same test. Your actual studying should be done in as isolated an environment as possible, but the work of organizing the information and setting up the study plan can be divided up. In between study sessions, you can discuss with your teammates the concepts that you're all studying and quiz each other on the details. Just be sure that your teammates are as serious about the test as you are. If you find that your study time is being replaced with social time, you might need to find a new team.

Strategy #2 – Make Your Studying Count

You're devoting a lot of time and effort to preparing for this test, so you want to be absolutely certain it will pay off. This means doing more than just reading the content and hoping you can remember it on test day. It's important to make every minute of study count. There are two main areas you can focus on to make your studying count.

Retention

It doesn't matter how much time you study if you can't remember the material. You need to make sure you are retaining the concepts. To check your retention of the information you're learning, try recalling it at later times with minimal prompting. Try carrying around flashcards and glance at one or two from time to time or ask a friend who's also studying for the test to quiz you.

To enhance your retention, look for ways to put the information into practice so that you can apply it rather than simply recalling it. If you're using the information in practical ways, it will be much easier to remember. Similarly, it helps to solidify a concept in your mind if you're not only reading it to yourself but also explaining it to someone else. Ask a friend to let you teach them about a concept you're a little shaky on (or speak aloud to an imaginary audience if necessary). As you try to summarize, define, give examples, and answer your friend's questions, you'll understand the concepts better and they will stay with you longer. Finally, step back for a big picture view and ask yourself how each piece of information fits with the whole subject. When you link the different concepts together and see them working together as a whole, it's easier to remember the individual components.

Finally, practice showing your work on any multi-step problems, even if you're just studying. Writing out each step you take to solve a problem will help solidify the process in your mind, and you'll be more likely to remember it during the test.

Modality

Modality simply refers to the means or method by which you study. Choosing a study modality that fits your own individual learning style is crucial. No two people learn best in exactly the same way, so it's important to know your strengths and use them to your advantage.

For example, if you learn best by visualization, focus on visualizing a concept in your mind and draw an image or a diagram. Try color-coding your notes, illustrating them, or creating symbols that will trigger your mind to recall a learned concept. If you learn best by hearing or discussing information, find a study partner who learns the same way or read aloud to yourself. Think about how to put the information in your own words. Imagine that you are giving a lecture on the topic and record yourself so you can listen to it later.

For any learning style, flashcards can be helpful. Organize the information so you can take advantage of spare moments to review. Underline key words or phrases. Use different colors for different categories. Mnemonic devices (such as creating a short list in which every item starts with the same letter) can also help with retention. Find what works best for you and use it to store the information in your mind most effectively and easily.

Strategy #3 – Practice the Right Way

Your success on test day depends not only on how many hours you put into preparing, but also on whether you prepared the right way. It's good to check along the way to see if your studying is paying off. One of the most effective ways to do this is by taking practice tests to evaluate your progress. Practice tests are useful because they show exactly where you need to improve. Every time you take a practice test, pay special attention to these three groups of questions:

- The questions you got wrong
- The questions you had to guess on, even if you guessed right
- The questions you found difficult or slow to work through

This will show you exactly what your weak areas are, and where you need to devote more study time. Ask yourself why each of these questions gave you trouble. Was it because you didn't understand the material? Was it because you didn't remember the vocabulary? Do you need more repetitions on this type of question to build speed and confidence? Dig into those questions and figure out how you can strengthen your weak areas as you go back to review the material.

Additionally, many practice tests have a section explaining the answer choices. It can be tempting to read the explanation and think that you now have a good understanding of the concept. However, an explanation likely only covers part of the question's broader context. Even if the explanation makes perfect sense, **go back and investigate** every concept related to the question until you're positive you have a thorough understanding.

As you go along, keep in mind that the practice test is just that: practice. Memorizing these questions and answers will not be very helpful on the actual test because it is unlikely to have any of the same exact questions. If you only know the right answers to the sample questions, you won't be prepared for the real thing. **Study the concepts** until you understand them fully, and then you'll be able to answer any question that shows up on the test.

It's important to wait on the practice tests until you're ready. If you take a test on your first day of study, you may be overwhelmed by the amount of material covered and how much you need to learn. Work up to it gradually.

On test day, you'll need to be prepared for answering questions, managing your time, and using the test-taking strategies you've learned. It's a lot to balance, like a mental marathon that will have a big impact on your future. Like training for a marathon, you'll need to start slowly and work your way up. When test day arrives, you'll be ready.

Start with the strategies you've read in the first two Success Strategies—plan your course and study in the way that works best for you. If you have time, consider using multiple study resources to get different approaches to the same concepts. It can be helpful to see difficult concepts from more than one angle. Then find a good source for practice tests. Many times, the test website will suggest potential study resources or provide sample tests.

Practice Test Strategy

If you're able to find at least three practice tests, we recommend this strategy:

Untimed and Open-Book Practice

Take the first test with no time constraints and with your notes and study guide handy. Take your time and focus on applying the strategies you've learned.

Timed and Open-Book Practice

Take the second practice test open-book as well, but set a timer and practice pacing yourself to finish in time.

Timed and Closed-Book Practice

Take any other practice tests as if it were test day. Set a timer and put away your study materials. Sit at a table or desk in a quiet room, imagine yourself at the testing center, and answer questions as quickly and accurately as possible.

Keep repeating timed and closed-book tests on a regular basis until you run out of practice tests or it's time for the actual test. Your mind will be ready for the schedule and stress of test day, and you'll be able to focus on recalling the material you've learned.

Strategy #4 – Pace Yourself

Once you're fully prepared for the material on the test, your biggest challenge on test day will be managing your time. Just knowing that the clock is ticking can make you panic even if you have plenty of time left. Work on pacing yourself so you can build confidence against the time constraints of the exam. Pacing is a difficult skill to master, especially in a high-pressure environment, so **practice is vital**.

Set time expectations for your pace based on how much time is available. For example, if a section has 60 questions and the time limit is 30 minutes, you know you have to average 30 seconds or less per question in order to answer them all. Although 30 seconds is the hard limit, set 25 seconds per question as your goal, so you reserve extra time to spend on harder questions. When you budget extra time for the harder questions, you no longer have any reason to stress when those questions take longer to answer.

Don't let this time expectation distract you from working through the test at a calm, steady pace, but keep it in mind so you don't spend too much time on any one question. Recognize that taking extra time on one question you don't understand may keep you from answering two that you do understand later in the test. If your time limit for a question is up and you're still not sure of the answer, mark it and move on, and come back to it later if the time and the test format allow. If the testing format doesn't allow you to return to earlier questions, just make an educated guess; then put it out of your mind and move on.

On the easier questions, be careful not to rush. It may seem wise to hurry through them so you have more time for the challenging ones, but it's not worth missing one if you know the concept and just didn't take the time to read the question fully. Work efficiently but make sure you understand the question and have looked at all of the answer choices, since more than one may seem right at first.

Even if you're paying attention to the time, you may find yourself a little behind at some point. You should speed up to get back on track, but do so wisely. Don't panic; just take a few seconds less on each question until you're caught up. Don't guess without thinking, but do look through the answer choices and eliminate any you know are wrong. If you can get down to two choices, it is often worthwhile to guess from those. Once you've chosen an answer, move on and don't dwell on any that you skipped or had to hurry through. If a question was taking too long, chances are it was one of the harder ones, so you weren't as likely to get it right anyway.

On the other hand, if you find yourself getting ahead of schedule, it may be beneficial to slow down a little. The more quickly you work, the more likely you are to make a careless mistake that will affect your score. You've budgeted time for each question, so don't be afraid to spend that time. Practice an efficient but careful pace to get the most out of the time you have.

Test-Taking Strategies

This section contains a list of test-taking strategies that you may find helpful as you work through the test. By taking what you know and applying logical thought, you can maximize your chances of answering any question correctly!

It is very important to realize that every question is different and every person is different: no single strategy will work on every question, and no single strategy will work for every person. That's why we've included all of them here, so you can try them out and determine which ones work best for different types of questions and which ones work best for you.

Question Strategies

✓ Read Carefully

Read the question and the answer choices carefully. Don't miss the question because you misread the terms. You have plenty of time to read each question thoroughly and make sure you understand what is being asked. Yet a happy medium must be attained, so don't waste too much time. You must read carefully and efficiently.

✓ Contextual Clues

Look for contextual clues. If the question includes a word you are not familiar with, look at the immediate context for some indication of what the word might mean. Contextual clues can often give you all the information you need to decipher the meaning of an unfamiliar word. Even if you can't determine the meaning, you may be able to narrow down the possibilities enough to make a solid guess at the answer to the question.

✓ Prefixes

If you're having trouble with a word in the question or answer choices, try dissecting it. Take advantage of every clue that the word might include. Prefixes can be a huge help. Usually, they allow you to determine a basic meaning. *Pre-* means before, *post-* means after, *pro-* is positive, *de-* is negative. From prefixes, you can get an idea of the general meaning of the word and try to put it into context.

✓ Hedge Words

Watch out for critical hedge words, such as *likely, may, can, often, almost, mostly, usually, generally, rarely,* and *sometimes.* Question writers insert these hedge phrases to cover every possibility. Often an answer choice will be wrong simply because it leaves no room for exception. Be on guard for answer choices that have definitive words such as *exactly* and *always.*

✓ Switchback Words

Stay alert for *switchbacks.* These are the words and phrases frequently used to alert you to shifts in thought. The most common switchback words are *but, although,* and *however.* Others include *nevertheless, on the other hand, even though, while, in spite of, despite,* and *regardless of.* Switchback words are important to catch because they can change the direction of the question or an answer choice.

☑ FACE VALUE

When in doubt, use common sense. Accept the situation in the problem at face value. Don't read too much into it. These problems will not require you to make wild assumptions. If you have to go beyond creativity and warp time or space in order to have an answer choice fit the question, then you should move on and consider the other answer choices. These are normal problems rooted in reality. The applicable relationship or explanation may not be readily apparent, but it is there for you to figure out. Use your common sense to interpret anything that isn't clear.

Answer Choice Strategies

☑ ANSWER SELECTION

The most thorough way to pick an answer choice is to identify and eliminate wrong answers until only one is left, then confirm it is the correct answer. Sometimes an answer choice may immediately seem right, but be careful. The test writers will usually put more than one reasonable answer choice on each question, so take a second to read all of them and make sure that the other choices are not equally obvious. As long as you have time left, it is better to read every answer choice than to pick the first one that looks right without checking the others.

☑ ANSWER CHOICE FAMILIES

An answer choice family consists of two (in rare cases, three) answer choices that are very similar in construction and cannot all be true at the same time. If you see two answer choices that are direct opposites or parallels, one of them is usually the correct answer. For instance, if one answer choice says that quantity *x* increases and another either says that quantity *x* decreases (opposite) or says that quantity *y* increases (parallel), then those answer choices would fall into the same family. An answer choice that doesn't match the construction of the answer choice family is more likely to be incorrect. Most questions will not have answer choice families, but when they do appear, you should be prepared to recognize them.

☑ ELIMINATE ANSWERS

Eliminate answer choices as soon as you realize they are wrong, but make sure you consider all possibilities. If you are eliminating answer choices and realize that the last one you are left with is also wrong, don't panic. Start over and consider each choice again. There may be something you missed the first time that you will realize on the second pass.

☑ AVOID FACT TRAPS

Don't be distracted by an answer choice that is factually true but doesn't answer the question. You are looking for the choice that answers the question. Stay focused on what the question is asking for so you don't accidentally pick an answer that is true but incorrect. Always go back to the question and make sure the answer choice you've selected actually answers the question and is not merely a true statement.

☑ EXTREME STATEMENTS

In general, you should avoid answers that put forth extreme actions as standard practice or proclaim controversial ideas as established fact. An answer choice that states the "process should be used in certain situations, if..." is much more likely to be correct than one that states the "process should be discontinued completely." The first is a calm rational statement and doesn't even make a definitive, uncompromising stance, using a hedge word *if* to provide wiggle room, whereas the second choice is far more extreme.

✓ Benchmark

As you read through the answer choices and you come across one that seems to answer the question well, mentally select that answer choice. This is not your final answer, but it's the one that will help you evaluate the other answer choices. The one that you selected is your benchmark or standard for judging each of the other answer choices. Every other answer choice must be compared to your benchmark. That choice is correct until proven otherwise by another answer choice beating it. If you find a better answer, then that one becomes your new benchmark. Once you've decided that no other choice answers the question as well as your benchmark, you have your final answer.

✓ Predict the Answer

Before you even start looking at the answer choices, it is often best to try to predict the answer. When you come up with the answer on your own, it is easier to avoid distractions and traps because you will know exactly what to look for. The right answer choice is unlikely to be word-for-word what you came up with, but it should be a close match. Even if you are confident that you have the right answer, you should still take the time to read each option before moving on.

General Strategies

✓ Tough Questions

If you are stumped on a problem or it appears too hard or too difficult, don't waste time. Move on! Remember though, if you can quickly check for obviously incorrect answer choices, your chances of guessing correctly are greatly improved. Before you completely give up, at least try to knock out a couple of possible answers. Eliminate what you can and then guess at the remaining answer choices before moving on.

✓ Check Your Work

Since you will probably not know every term listed and the answer to every question, it is important that you get credit for the ones that you do know. Don't miss any questions through careless mistakes. If at all possible, try to take a second to look back over your answer selection and make sure you've selected the correct answer choice and haven't made a costly careless mistake (such as marking an answer choice that you didn't mean to mark). This quick double check should more than pay for itself in caught mistakes for the time it costs.

✓ Pace Yourself

It's easy to be overwhelmed when you're looking at a page full of questions; your mind is confused and full of random thoughts, and the clock is ticking down faster than you would like. Calm down and maintain the pace that you have set for yourself. Especially as you get down to the last few minutes of the test, don't let the small numbers on the clock make you panic. As long as you are on track by monitoring your pace, you are guaranteed to have time for each question.

✓ Don't Rush

It is very easy to make errors when you are in a hurry. Maintaining a fast pace in answering questions is pointless if it makes you miss questions that you would have gotten right otherwise. Test writers like to include distracting information and wrong answers that seem right. Taking a little extra time to avoid careless mistakes can make all the difference in your test score. Find a pace that allows you to be confident in the answers that you select.

⊘ Keep Moving

Panicking will not help you pass the test, so do your best to stay calm and keep moving. Taking deep breaths and going through the answer elimination steps you practiced can help to break through a stress barrier and keep your pace.

Final Notes

The combination of a solid foundation of content knowledge and the confidence that comes from practicing your plan for applying that knowledge is the key to maximizing your performance on test day. As your foundation of content knowledge is built up and strengthened, you'll find that the strategies included in this chapter become more and more effective in helping you quickly sift through the distractions and traps of the test to isolate the correct answer.

Now that you're preparing to move forward into the test content chapters of this book, be sure to keep your goal in mind. As you read, think about how you will be able to apply this information on the test. If you've already seen sample questions for the test and you have an idea of the question format and style, try to come up with questions of your own that you can answer based on what you're reading. This will give you valuable practice applying your knowledge in the same ways you can expect to on test day.

Good luck and good studying!

Physical Science

Basic Organization of Matter

An **element** is the most basic type of matter. It has unique properties and cannot be broken down into other elements. The smallest unit of an element is the **atom**. A chemical combination of two or more types of elements is called a compound. **Compounds** often have properties that are very different from those of their constituent elements. The smallest independent unit of an element or compound is known as a **molecule**. Most elements are found somewhere in nature in single-atom form, but a few elements only exist naturally in pairs. These are called diatomic elements, of which some of the most common are hydrogen, nitrogen, and oxygen. Elements and compounds are represented by chemical symbols, one or two letters, most often the first in the element name. More than one atom of the same element in a compound is represented with a subscript number designating how many atoms of that element are present. Water, for instance, contains two hydrogens and one oxygen. Thus, the chemical formula is H_2O. Methane contains one carbon and four hydrogens, so its formula is CH_4.

Atom

A **neutral atom** consists of an extremely dense **nucleus** composed of one or more positively-charged **protons** and a varying number of uncharged **neutrons**, except for hydrogen-1 which contains no neutrons, surrounded by a cloud of one or more negatively-charged **electrons**. This cloud is also called the **electron cloud**. In a neutral atom, the number of electrons equals the number of protons in the nucleus. The protons and neutrons are bound together by the strong nuclear force, which overcomes the repulsive force the positive charges of the protons have for each other. The negatively-charged electrons are bound to the positively-charged protons by the attractive electromagnetic force. The number of protons, or the atomic number, determines the chemical element the atom represents. The number of electrons in the outermost shell determines how the atom interacts with other atoms or molecules.

Protons, Neutrons, and Electrons

The three major subatomic particles are the proton, neutron, and electron. The **proton**, which is located in the nucleus, has a relative charge of +1. The **neutron**, which is located in the nucleus, has a relative charge of 0. The **electron**, which is located outside the nucleus, has a relative charge of –1. The proton and neutron, which are essentially the same mass, are much more massive than the electron and make up the mass of the atom. The electron's mass is insignificant compared to the mass of the proton and neutron.

Review Video: Structure of Atoms
Visit mometrix.com/academy and enter code: 905932

EXAMPLE

Neon is a chemical element belonging to the Noble Gases, which have very low reactivity. A typical neon atom contains 10 protons, 10 neutrons, and 10 electrons. Which of the following best explains why neon has such low reactivity?

a. It has an equal number of protons, neutrons, and electrons.
b. It has a full outer electron shell.
c. It has an empty outer electron shell.
d. It has an overall charge of zero.

Choice A states that having an equal number of protons, neutrons, and electrons makes an atom more stable. However, most atoms have a balanced number of protons and electrons, and many have the same number of neutrons as well. This does not explain neon's low reactivity, making it incorrect.

Choice B states that neon has a full outer electron shell. When atoms react with one another, they do so to gain or lose electrons. Having a full outer shell makes an element less reactive because it does not need to bond with another atom in order to have a stable number of electrons. This could be the correct answer.

Choice C states that neon has an empty outer electron shell. Having a full outer shell makes an element less reactive, so this does not make sense. This answer is incorrect.

Choice D states that neon has an overall charge of zero. This is true because the charge of the protons and the charge of the electrons cancel one another out. However, reactivity is a result of how many electrons are in an element's outer shell and is unrelated to its overall charge.

Choice B is the correct answer because the number of electrons in an atom's outer shell is the most important factor in the element's reactivity. Because neon has a full outer electron shell, it is unlikely to react with other elements.

Atomic Number and Mass Number

The **atomic number** of an element is the number of protons in the nucleus of an atom of that element. This is the number that identifies the type of an atom. For example, all oxygen atoms have eight protons, and all carbon atoms have six protons. Each element is identified by its specific atomic number.

The **mass number** is the number of protons and neutrons in the nucleus of an atom. Although the atomic number is the same for all atoms of a specific element, the mass number can vary due to the varying numbers of neutrons in various isotopes of the atom.

Example

An atom has an atomic mass of 81, 40 protons, and an overall neutral charge. Which of the following configurations is possible?

a. 40 protons, 40 neutrons, 40 electrons
b. 40 protons, 41 neutrons, 40 electrons
c. 40 protons, 41 neutrons, 41 electrons
d. 40 protons, 40 neutrons, 41 electrons

Choice A proposes that the atom would contain 40 neutrons and 40 electrons. The information given in the prompt explains that the atomic mass of the atom is 81 atomic mass units (AMU). Because we know the number of protons is 40, we can find the number of neutrons by subtracting 40 from 81, resulting in 41. Choice A is incorrect because the atom would have 41 neutrons rather than 40.

Choice B proposes an atom with 41 neutrons and 40 electrons. The atomic mass of an atom with 40 protons and 41 neutrons is 81, matching the atomic mass in the description. The atom should also have an overall neutral charge. Since the positive and negative charges of protons and electrons cancel out, a neutral atom would have 40 electrons. Choice B has the correct number of neutrons and electrons.

Choice C proposes an atom with 41 neutrons and 41 electrons. As shown above, an atom with 41 neutrons would have the given atomic mass. However, an atom with 40 protons and 41 electrons would have an overall charge of negative 1. Choice C is incorrect.

Choice D proposes an atom with 40 neutrons and 41 electrons. This does not match the atomic mass or overall charge of the atom described in the question, so Choice D is incorrect.

Choice B is the correct answer because it is the only atomic configuration that results in an atomic mass of 81 and an overall neutral charge.

Elements, Compounds, Solutions, and Mixtures

- **Elements** — An element is matter with one particular type of atom. It can be identified by its atomic number or the number of protons in its nucleus. There are approximately 118 elements currently known, 94 of which occur naturally on Earth. Elements from the periodic table include hydrogen, carbon, iron, helium, mercury, and oxygen.
- **Compounds** — These are substances containing two or more elements. Compounds are formed by chemical reactions and frequently have different properties than the original elements. Compounds are decomposed by a chemical reaction rather than separated by a physical one.
- **Solutions** — These are homogeneous mixtures composed of two or more substances that have become one.
- **Mixtures** — Mixtures contain two or more substances that are combined but have not reacted chemically with each other. Mixtures can be separated using physical methods, while compounds cannot.

Review Video: Pure Substances and Mixtures
Visit mometrix.com/academy and enter code: 100384

Interaction of Atoms to Form Compounds

Atoms interact by **transferring** or sharing the electrons furthest from the nucleus. Known as the outer or **valence electrons**, they are responsible for the chemical properties of an element. **Bonds** between atoms are created when electrons are paired up by being transferred or shared. If electrons are transferred from one atom to another, the bond is ionic. If electrons are shared, the bond is covalent. Atoms of the same element may bond together to form molecules or crystalline solids. When two or more different types of atoms bind together chemically, a compound is made. The physical properties of compounds reflect the nature of the interactions among their molecules. These interactions are determined by the structure of the molecule, including the atoms they consist of and the distances and angles between them.

Periodic Table

The **periodic table** groups elements with similar chemical properties together. The grouping of elements is based on atomic structure. It shows periodic trends of physical and chemical properties and identifies families of elements with similar properties. It is a common model for organizing and understanding elements. In the periodic table, each element has its own cell that includes varying amounts of information presented in symbol form about the properties of the element. Cells in the table are arranged in rows (periods) and columns (groups or families). At minimum, a cell includes the symbol for the element and its atomic number. The cell for hydrogen, for example, which appears first in the upper left corner, includes an "H" and a "1" above the letter. Elements are ordered by atomic number, left to right, top to bottom.

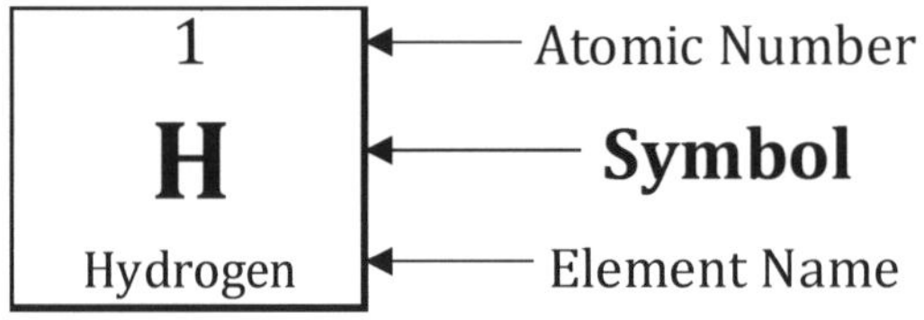

Review Video: Periodic Table
Visit mometrix.com/academy and enter code: 154828

In the periodic table, the groups are the columns numbered 1 through 18 that group elements with similar outer electron shell configurations. Since the configuration of the outer electron shell is one of the primary factors affecting an element's chemical properties, elements within the same group have similar chemical properties. Previous naming conventions for groups have included the use of Roman numerals and upper-case letters. Currently, the periodic table groups are: Group 1, alkali metals; Group 2, alkaline earth metals; Groups 3-12, transition metals; Group 13, boron family; Group 14; carbon family; Group 15, pnictogens; Group 16, chalcogens; Group 17, halogens; Group 18, noble gases.

In the periodic table, there are seven periods (rows), and within each period there are blocks that group elements with the same outer electron subshell (more on this in the next section). The number of electrons in that outer shell determines which group an element belongs to within a given block. Each row's number (1, 2, 3, etc.) corresponds to the highest number electron shell that is in use. For example, row 2 uses only electron shells 1 and 2, while row 7 uses all shells from 1-7.

Groups and Periods in the Periodic Table

A **group** is a vertical column of the periodic table. Elements in the same group have the same number of **valence electrons.** For the representative elements, the number of valence electrons is equal to the group number. Because of their equal valence electrons, elements in the same groups have similar physical and chemical properties. A period is a horizontal row of the periodic table. Atomic number increases from left to right across a row. The **period** of an element corresponds to the **highest energy level** of the electrons in the atoms of that element. The energy level increases from top to bottom down a group.

Period ↓ / Group →	1	2	3	4	5	6	7	8	9	10	11	12	13	14	15	16	17	18
1	1 H																	2 He
2	3 Li	4 Be											5 B	6 C	7 N	8 O	9 F	10 Ne
3	11 Na	12 Mg											13 Al	14 Si	15 P	16 S	17 Cl	18 Ar
4	19 K	20 Ca	21 Sc	22 Ti	23 V	24 Cr	25 Mn	26 Fe	27 Co	28 Ni	29 Cu	30 Zn	31 Ga	32 Ge	33 As	34 Se	35 Br	36 Kr
5	37 Rb	38 Sr	39 Y	40 Zr	41 Nb	42 Mo	43 Tc	44 Ru	45 Rh	46 Pd	47 Ag	48 Cd	49 In	50 Sn	51 Sb	52 Te	53 I	54 Xe
6	55 Cs	56 Ba	*	72 Hf	73 Ta	74 W	75 Re	76 Os	77 Ir	78 Pt	79 Au	80 Hg	81 Tl	82 Pb	83 Bi	84 Po	85 At	86 Rn
7	87 Fr	88 Ra	**	104 Rf	105 Db	106 Sg	107 Bh	108 Hs	109 Mt	110 Ds	111 Rg	112 Cn	113 Uut	114 Fl	115 Uup	116 Lv	117 Uus	118 Uuo

*	57 La	58 Ce	59 Pr	60 Nd	61 Pm	62 Sm	63 Eu	64 Gd	65 Tb	66 Dy	67 Ho	68 Er	69 Tm	70 Yb	71 Lu
**	89 Ac	90 Th	91 Pa	92 U	93 Np	94 Pu	95 Am	96 Cm	97 Bk	98 Cf	99 Es	100 Fm	101 Md	102 No	103 Lr

Atomic Number and Atomic Mass in the Periodic Table

The elements in the periodic table are arranged in order of **increasing atomic number** first left to right and then top to bottom across the periodic table. The **atomic number** represents the number of protons in the atoms of that element. Because of the increasing numbers of protons, the atomic mass typically also increases from left to right across a period and from top to bottom down a row. The **atomic mass** is a weighted average of all the naturally occurring isotopes of an element.

Using Mass and Density to Identify an Unknown Substance

Density is a **physical property** that measures how much matter is contained within a certain amount of space. Different substances have their own unique densities, which means scientists can determine the identity of an unknown substance by calculating its density. Density is calculated using the equation **density = mass / volume. Mass** can easily be measured using tools like a triple-beam balance. Finding the **volume** of a substance depends on its phase of matter. For example, to calculate the volume of a liquid, scientists use glassware such as a graduated cylinder. However, to calculate the volume of a solid, scientists use equations based on the shape of the sample. They can also submerge the sample in water and calculate how much the volume has changed, which is called the **water displacement method**. Using measurements for mass and volume along with the equation above, scientists can calculate an unknown substance's density and compare it to the average densities of known substances in order to identify it. For example, a substance with a density of 2.7 g/cm^3 is likely to be aluminum, while a value of 11.3 g/cm^3 is likely to be lead.

ATOMIC SYMBOLS

The **atomic symbol** for many elements is simply the first letter of the element name. For example, the atomic symbol for hydrogen is H, and the atomic symbol for carbon is C. The atomic symbol of other elements is the first two letters of the element name. For example, the atomic symbol for helium is He, and the atomic symbol for cobalt is Co. The atomic symbols of several elements are derived from Latin. For example, the atomic symbol for copper (Cu) is derived from *cuprum,* and the atomic symbol for iron (Fe) is derived from *ferrum.* The atomic symbol for tungsten (W) is derived from the German word *wolfram*.

ARRANGEMENT OF METALS, NONMETALS, AND METALLOIDS IN THE PERIODIC TABLE

The **metals** are located on the left side and center of the periodic table, and the **nonmetals** are located on the right side of the periodic table. The **metalloids** or **semimetals** form a zigzag line between the metals and nonmetals as shown below. Metals include the alkali metals such as lithium, sodium, and potassium and the alkaline earth metals such as beryllium, magnesium, and calcium. Metals also include the transition metals such as iron, copper, and nickel and the inner transition metals such as thorium, uranium, and plutonium. Nonmetals include the chalcogens such as oxygen and sulfur, the halogens such as fluorine and chlorine, and the noble gases such as helium and argon. Carbon, nitrogen, and phosphorus are also nonmetals. Metalloids or semimetals include boron, silicon, germanium, antimony, and polonium.

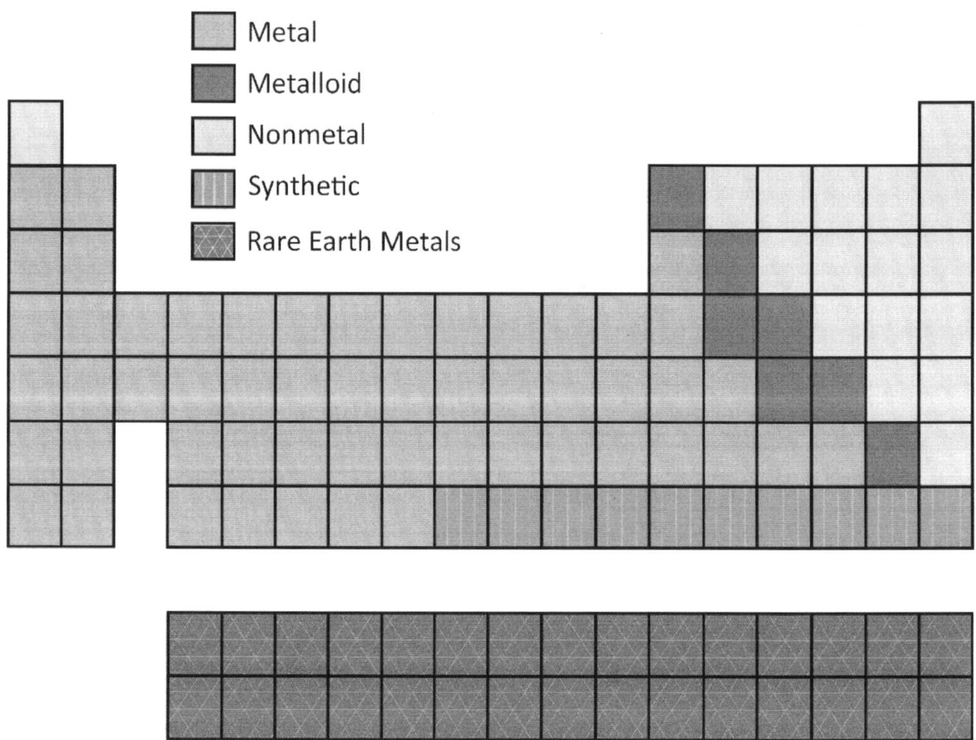

ARRANGEMENT OF TRANSITION ELEMENTS

The **transition elements** belong to one of two categories—transition metals or inner transition metals. The **transition metals** are located in the middle of the periodic table, and the inner transition metals are typically set off as two rows by themselves at the bottom of the periodic table. The transition metals correspond to the "*d* block" for orbital filling, and the inner transition metals correspond to the "*f* block" for orbital filling. Examples of transition metals include iron, copper, nickel, and zinc. The inner transition metals consist of the *lanthanide* or *rare-earth series*, which corresponds to the first row, and the *actinide series*, which corresponds to the second row of the inner transition metals. The *lanthanide series* includes lanthanum, cerium, and praseodymium. The *actinide series* includes actinium, uranium, and plutonium.

Physical Properties of the Elements in Relation to the Periodic Table

The **boiling point**, **melting point**, and **conductivity** of the elements depend partially on the number of valence electrons of the atoms of those elements. For the representative elements in groups 1A–8A, the number of valence electrons matches the group number. Because all of the elements in each individual group contain the same number of valence electrons, elements in the same groups tend to have similar boiling points, melting points, and conductivity. Boiling points and melting points tend to decrease moving down the column of groups 1A–4A and 8A but increase slightly moving down the column of groups 5A–7A.

Physical Properties of Metals, Nonmetals, and Metalloids

The periodic table separates elements based on the physical and chemical properties of their pure forms. Elements fall into one of three categories based on their properties: **metals**, **nonmetals**, or **metalloids**. One of these key properties is **luster**, which describes how well a material reflects light. Other examples include **conductivity**, or how easily the material conducts heat or electricity, and **malleability**, meaning how easily the material can be molded and shaped. Metals, such as copper and gold, are easily identified as having high luster, high conductivity, and high malleability. Comparatively, solid nonmetals are dull or low luster, poor conductors, and easily break when bent. Lastly, metalloids are substances that possess a combination of the properties that are characteristic of metals and nonmetals. For example, silicon has high luster like a metal, is a moderate conductor of electricity, and has a brittle consistency like that of a nonmetal.

Chemical Reactivity in Relation to the Periodic Table

Atoms of elements in the same **group** or **family** of the periodic table tend to have **similar chemical properties** and **similar chemical reactions**. For example, the alkali metals, which form cations with a charge of +1, tend to react with water to form hydrogen gas and metal hydroxides. The alkaline earth metals, which form cations with a charge of +2, react with oxygen gas to form metal oxides. The halogens, which form anions with a charge of −1, are highly reactive and toxic. The noble gases are unreactive and never form compounds naturally.

Example

Copper (atomic number 29), silver (atomic number 47), and gold (atomic number 79) are soft and shiny metals that are useful for creating coins, jewelry, and electrical wiring. Which of the following explains these metals' shared properties?

a. They belong to the same period of the periodic table.
b. They belong to the same group of the periodic table.
c. They contain the same number of protons.
d. They contain the same number of total electrons.

Choice A states that these elements belong to the same period of the periodic table, resulting in their similar properties. A period, or row, on the periodic table is organized by atomic number. For example, copper is followed by zinc (30) and gallium (31). Elements in the same period do not share the same properties. Thus, choice A is incorrect.

Choice B states that these three elements belong to the same group. A group on the periodic table is a vertical column of elements that share similar properties. Elements are grouped based on how many electrons exist in their outer shell, which influences the properties of the element. If copper, silver, and gold were in the same group, then it would make sense that they share properties. Choice B could be the answer.

Choice C states that these elements have the same number of protons. An element's number of protons is equal to its atomic number, which is different for each element. For example, copper has 29 protons, making its atomic number 29. It is impossible for three different elements to have the same number of protons, so choice C is incorrect.

Choice D states that the elements contain the same number of total electrons. For a neutral atom, the number of electrons is equal to the number of protons. In this case, copper should have 29 electrons while silver should have 47. Copper, silver, and gold do have the same number of electrons in their outer shell. However, this answer specifies "total electrons," making it incorrect. Choice D is not the answer.

Choice B is the correct answer because elements in the same group of the periodic table share similar properties.

Chemical Formulas

A chemical formula is a set of letters, numbers, and symbols that describe the elemental composition of a particular substance. Elements are listed by their periodic table symbol. A subscript number after the element symbol indicates the number of that type of element's atoms in the formula. If there is no subscript, there is only one atom of that type of element. There are three common types of chemical formulas to be familiar with:

1. The *molecular formula* describes the elemental composition of a single molecule of a substance. For instance, the molecular formula for glucose is $C_6H_{12}O_6$, because each molecule of glucose contains six atoms of carbon and oxygen, and twelve atoms of hydrogen.
2. The *empirical formula* is a reduced form of the molecular formula that gives only the ratios of the elements in a substance. For instance, the empirical formula for glucose is CH_2O, because the ratio of carbon to hydrogen to oxygen in glucose is 1 to 2 to 1. The empirical formula will be the same as the molecular formula for many simple substances.
3. The *structural formula* is an expanded formula that gives information about the way that the atoms in a molecule are bonded. Below is an example of the structural formula for ethane:

```
    H   H
    |   |
H — C — C — H
    |   |
    H   H
```

EXAMPLE

Sulfuric acid is a strong acid composed of hydrogen, sulfur, and oxygen atoms. The chemical formula for sulfuric acid is H_2SO_4. Which of the following correctly describes the number of hydrogen, sulfur, and oxygen atoms in sulfuric acid?

a. 2 hydrogen; 4 sulfur; 4 oxygen
b. 2 hydrogen; 1 sulfur; 4 oxygen
c. 8 hydrogen; 1 sulfur; 4 oxygen
d. 8 hydrogen; 4 sulfur; 8 oxygen

Choice A: 2 hydrogen; 4 sulfur; 4 oxygen. When counting the number of atoms in a chemical formula, each element is represented by its atomic symbol. In this case, we have H, S, and O representing hydrogen, sulfur, and oxygen, respectively. The number next to the atomic symbol, called a subscript, denotes how many atoms of that element are in the molecule. In H_2SO_4, there is no subscript next to the S, which means there is only one sulfur atom. Choice A is incorrect because there is only one sulfur atom in sulfuric acid, not four.

Choice B: 2 hydrogen; 1 sulfur; 4 oxygen. This option has one sulfur atom, making it a possible correct answer. The number of hydrogen atoms is denoted next to the H in H_2SO_4. Therefore, there are 2 hydrogen atoms in H_2SO_4. Lastly, the four next to the O in H_2SO_4 means there are four oxygen atoms in H_2SO_4. In summary, H_2SO_4 consists of two hydrogen atoms, one sulfur atom, and four oxygen atoms. Choice B is correct.

Choice C: 8 hydrogen; 1 sulfur; 4 oxygen. This answer is incorrect because it does not have the correct number of hydrogen atoms. Choice C is not the answer.

Choice D: 8 hydrogen; 4 sulfur; 8 oxygen. This answer has the incorrect number of all three atoms. The subscript only affects the element directly before it. Choice D is not the answer.

Choice B is the answer because it has the correct number for all three elements. The subscript to the right of the element denotes how many atoms there are, and having no subscript means there is only one atom of that element.

Physical Changes

Physical changes are those that do not affect the chemical properties of a substance. Changes in state are **physical changes**. For example, a liquid can freeze into a solid or boil into a gas without changing the chemical nature of the substance. It is all still the same substance. Ice, steam, and liquid water are all still water, H_2O. Physical properties include such features as shape, texture, size, volume, mass, and density. Cutting, melting, dissolving, mixing, breaking, and crushing are all types of physical changes.

Chemical Changes

Chemical changes occur when chemical bonds are broken and new ones are formed. The original substances are **transformed** into different substances. If vinegar and baking soda are mixed together, a lot of bubbles (carbon dioxide) and water will form. Burning wood in a fireplace is another type of chemical change. The carbon in the wood reacts with oxygen in the air to make ash, carbon dioxide, smoke and energy that we feel as heat and see as light.

Examples of chemical changes include the following:

- (a) The temperature of a system changes without any heating or cooling.
- (b) The formation of a gas (bubbles).
- (c) The formation of a precipitate (solid) when two liquids are mixed.
- (d) A liquid changes color.

A **chemical change** occurs when two or more substances come together and interact in such a way that they become completely new substances. For example, two hydrogen atoms and one oxygen atom combine to make a new compound—a water molecule, H_2O. Likewise, two oxygen atoms and one carbon atom combine to make one molecule of carbon dioxide—CO_2. The two substances that combine are called **reactants,** and the new compound that emerges is the **product**. Chemical reactions (changes) can be much more complicated than this.

Chemical equation

Chemical equations describe chemical reactions. The reactants are on the left side before the arrow. The products are on the right side after the arrow. The arrow is the mark that points to the reaction or change. The coefficient is the number before the element. This gives the ratio of reactants to products in terms of moles.

The equation for making water from hydrogen and oxygen is $2H_{2(g)} + O_{2(g)} \rightarrow 2H_2O_{(l)}$. The number 2 before hydrogen and water is the coefficient. This means that there are 2 moles of hydrogen and 2 of water. There is 1 mole of oxygen. This does not need to have the number 1 before the symbol for the element. For additional information, the following subscripts are often included to indicate the state of the substance: (g) stands for gas, (l) stands for liquid, (s) stands for solid, and (aq) stands for aqueous. Aqueous means the substance is dissolved in water. Charges are shown by superscript for individual ions, not for ionic compounds. Polyatomic ions are separated by parentheses. This is done so the kind of ion will not be confused with the number of ions.

Review Video: The Process of a Reaction
Visit mometrix.com/academy and enter code: 808039

In a chemical equation, it is necessary to have the same number of atoms for each element on each side of the equation. Reactants appear on the left side of the equation and the products appear on the right. The elements are balanced by placing the necessary coefficients in front of each element or compound. In a simple example, diatomic hydrogen (H_2) combines with diatomic oxygen (O_2) to form water:

$$H_2 + O_2 \rightarrow H_2O$$

Adding up all the atoms for each element shows that there is one more oxygen on the reactant side than the product side of the equation. Since water contains twice as many hydrogen atoms as oxygen atoms, placing the coefficient 2 in front of both the hydrogen molecule on the reactant side and the water molecule on the product side balances the equation:

$$2\,H_2 + O_2 \rightarrow 2\,H_2O$$

Again, count the number of atoms of each element on both sides of the equation. There are 4 hydrogen atoms and 2 oxygen atoms on each side of the equation so it is balanced.

Review Video: Balancing Chemical Equations
Visit mometrix.com/academy and enter code: 341228

Law of Conservation of Mass

The **law of conservation of mass** is also known as the **law of conservation of matter**. This basically means that in a closed system, the total mass of the products must equal the total mass of the reactants. This could also be stated that in a closed system, mass never changes. A consequence of this law is that matter is never created or destroyed during a typical chemical reaction. The atoms of the reactants are simply rearranged to form the products. The number and type of each specific atom involved in the reactants is identical to the number and type of atoms in the products.

This is the key principle used when balancing chemical equations. In a balanced chemical equation, the number of moles of each element on the reactant side equals the number of moles of each element on the product side.

Law of Conservation of Energy

The **law of conservation of energy** states that in a closed system, energy cannot be created or destroyed but only changed from one form to another. This is also known as the first law of thermodynamics. Another way to state this is that the **total energy in an isolated system is constant**. Energy comes in many forms that may be transformed from one kind to another, but in a closed system, the total amount of energy is conserved or remains constant. For example, potential energy can be converted to kinetic energy, thermal energy, radiant energy, or mechanical energy. In an isolated chemical reaction, there can be no energy created or destroyed. The energy simply changes forms.

Example

A group of 8th-grade science students mixed 100 grams of blue copper (II) chloride solution ($CuCl_2$) with 1 gram of aluminum foil. Which of the following observations could be used as evidence that a chemical reaction occurred?

a. The reaction took 20 minutes.
b. The mass after the reaction occurred was 97 grams.
c. The reaction produced a copper-red crumbly solid.
d. A phase change did not occur.

Choice A: This answer describes how long the reaction takes, which is an example of a scientific observation and could be useful information. However, this information alone does not tell us whether or not a chemical reaction occurred. Choice A can be eliminated.

Choice B: This answer describes the mass of the reaction's products, which does not tell us whether or not a chemical reaction occurred. In addition, this piece of data shows that the mass of the products (97 grams) was less than the mass of the reactants (100 grams). Because chemical reactions follow the Law of Conservation of Mass, the mass before and after a chemical reaction must be the same. This choice does not provide evidence that a chemical reaction occurred.

Choice C: This option describes the product of the reaction, a copper-red crumbly solid. This is different from the reactants the students mixed together: a blue solution and aluminum foil, which is a shiny silver metal. The substance produced had different properties than the original substances, such as a new copper color and a crumbly texture. Chemical reactions always produce a new substance with different properties than the reactants, so this could be evidence that a chemical reaction occurred. Choice C might be the answer.

Choice D: This option states that a phase change did not occur. A phase change is the transformation from one state of matter to another, such as ice melting into water. While a phase change is not a chemical reaction, simply stating that a phase change did not occur does not necessarily mean that a chemical reaction did occur. This choice can be eliminated because it is not evidence of a chemical reaction.

Choice C is the best answer because it describes a new substance with different properties that was produced, indicating that a chemical reaction has occurred.

Conversion of Energy Within Chemical Systems

Chemical energy is the energy stored in molecules in the bonds between the atoms of those molecules and the energy associated with the intermolecular forces. This stored **potential energy** may be converted into **kinetic energy** and then into heat. During a chemical reaction, atoms may be rearranged and chemical bonds may be formed or broken accompanied by a corresponding absorption or release of energy, usually in the form of heat. According to the first law of thermodynamics, during these energy conversions, the **total amount of energy must be conserved**.

Life Science

Populations of Animals or Plants

A **population** consists of all of the **organisms** of a **certain kind** in a **defined area**, **region**, or **habitat**. It may be all the red foxes in a given national park, all the loblolly pines in Virginia (very hard to count), all the bullfrogs in a certain pond, or even all of the boxelder bugs on a single box elder tree. In the case of rare or endangered species it may be all of the individuals still living in the wild.

Several factors operate to keep animal and plant populations under control. Predation, grazing, disease, competition for limiting resources such as food or nutrients, water, habitat and living space, hunting and breeding territory, and sunlight for plants all play important roles. Even the size of the population can influence factors such as birth rate and severity of disease outbreaks or force individuals to migrate to other less crowded areas.

Abiotic and Biotic Factors

An ecosystem is a connected community of organisms that interact with one another as well as with their physical environment. Nonliving aspects of an organism's physical environment are called **abiotic factors**. Abiotic factors include things like water, air, soil, minerals, and sunlight. Animals drink water from sources such as streams and breathe in oxygen (O_2) from fresh air. Plants use their roots to obtain water and minerals from the soil. In addition, plants require sunlight and carbon dioxide (CO_2) from the air in order to carry out photosynthesis to live and grow. The living aspects of the ecosystem are called **biotic factors**. They include other organisms in that community, such as plants, animals, bacteria, fungi and protists.

Sources of Energy in Organisms

Energy flows in one direction: from the **sun**, through photosynthetic organisms such as green plants (producers) and algae (autotrophs), and then to herbivores, carnivores, and decomposers. **Autotrophs** are organisms capable of producing their own food. The organic molecules they produce are food for all other organisms (heterotrophs). **Producers** are green plants that manufacture food by photosynthesis. **Herbivores** are animals that eat only plants (deer, rabbits, etc.). Since they are the first animals to receive the energy captured by producers, herbivores are called primary consumers. **Carnivores**, or secondary consumers, are animals that eat the bodies of other animals for food. **Predators** (wolves, lions, etc.) kill other animals (prey), while scavengers consume animals that are already dead from predation or natural causes (buzzards). **Omnivores** are animals that eat both plants and other animals (humans). **Decomposers** include saprophytic fungi and bacteria that break down the complex structures of the bodies of living things into simpler forms that can be used by other living things. This recycling process releases energy from organic molecules.

Producers, Consumers, and Decomposers

Producers are organisms that can make their own food. Most producers are plants. Through photosynthesis plants make sugars that provide energy. Plants only need sunlight, water, and the proper minerals and other nutrients to live, grow, and reproduce themselves. **Consumers** are organisms that eat other organisms. Consumers are animals that eat plants or other animals that eat plants. **Decomposers** are organisms that feed on decaying plant and animal matter. Since decomposers cannot make their own food they are classified as consumers. Fungi such as mushrooms are *decomposers* that break down the tissues and wood of living or dead plants or the bodies of dead animals.

Mushrooms

Mushrooms are **fungi**, and most are **decomposers**, which is a special type of consumer. Fungi have no chlorophyll and cannot engage in photosynthesis. Therefore, they cannot produce their own food and must get it from other organisms. Mushrooms are the fruiting bodies of fungi which live in the ground or grow the roots or trunks of living or dead trees. Mushrooms produce spores, which like the seeds of plants produce new fungal colonies. Some fungi are parasites on plants or animals or even other fungi.

Herbivores, Carnivores, and Omnivores

Herbivores are animals that only eat plants. Examples are rabbits, deer, antelope, rhinoceroses and elephants. *Carnivores* are animals that only eat other animals, like lions, wolves, foxes, most bats, hawks and owls, insect-eating birds, snakes, and sharks. *Omnivores* are animals that eat both plants and other animals. Examples include bears, pigs, skunks, raccoons, birds like crows and ravens, and human beings.

Scavengers

Vultures are mostly *scavengers* that eat *carrion*— the dead and decaying flesh of animals. When an animal dies it immediately begins to decay or rot. Bacteria break down the dead tissues and release a foul smell that attracts scavengers like vultures, hyenas, crabs and lobsters, and certain flies that feed on decaying flesh. Many carnivores like coyotes, hyenas, opossums, hawks and eagles will also eat carrion in addition to catching live prey.

Energy Pyramid

Energy flow through an ecosystem can be tracked through an energy pyramid. An **energy pyramid** shows how energy is transferred from one trophic level to another. **Producers** always form the base of an energy pyramid, and the consumers form successive levels above the producers. Producers only store about 1% of the solar energy they receive. Then, each successive level only uses about 10% of the energy of the previous level. That means that **primary consumers** use about 10% of the energy used by primary producers, such as grasses and trees. Next, **secondary**

consumers use 10% of primary consumers' 10%, or 1% overall. This continues up for as many trophic levels as exist in a particular ecosystem.

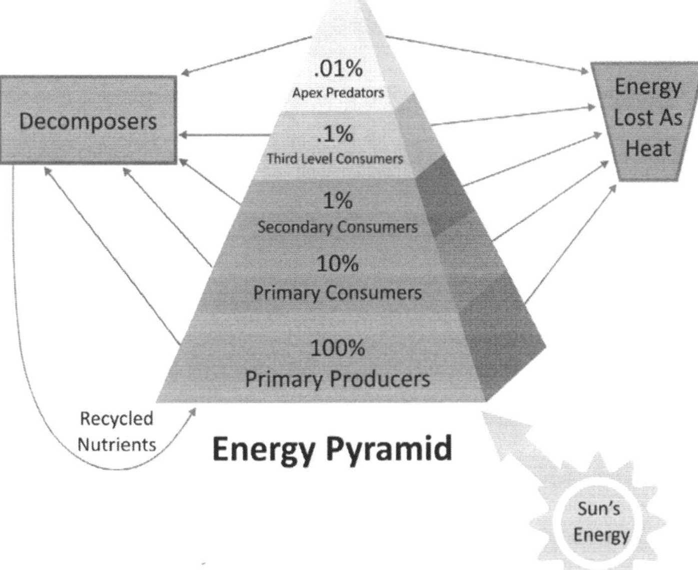

Food Web

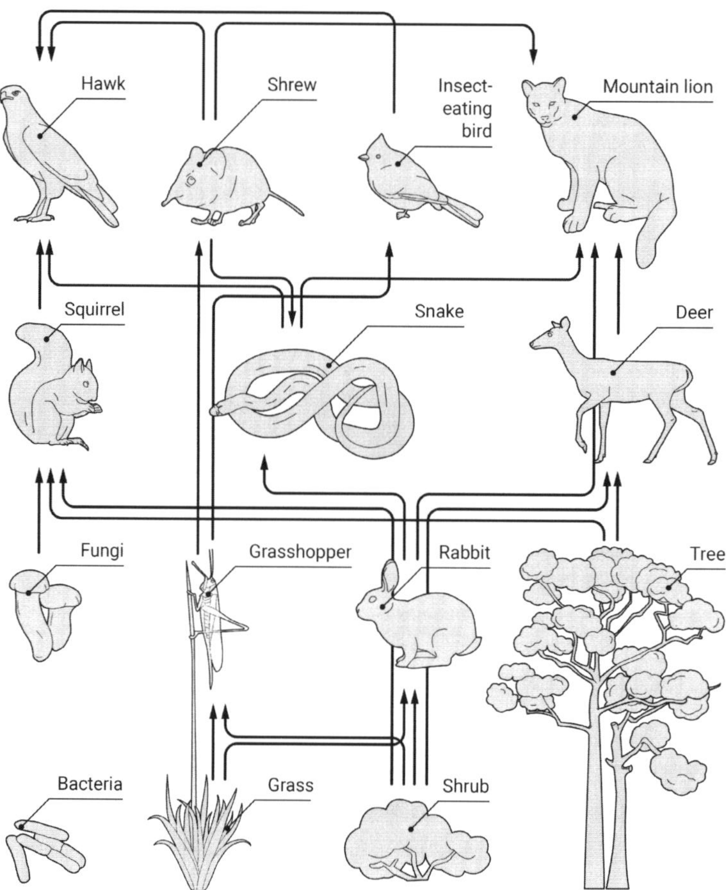

Energy flow through an ecosystem can be illustrated by a **food web**. Energy moves through the food web in the direction of the arrows. In the food web, **producers** such as grass, trees, and shrubs use energy from the Sun to produce food through photosynthesis. **Herbivores** or **primary consumers** such as squirrels, grasshoppers, and rabbits obtain energy by eating the producers. **Secondary consumers**, which are carnivores such as snakes and shrews, obtain energy by eating the primary consumers. **Tertiary consumers**, which are carnivores such as hawks and mountain lions, obtain energy by eating the secondary consumers.

> **Review Video: Food Webs**
> Visit mometrix.com/academy and enter code: 853254

Interdependence of the Food Web

Because each level of consumer is dependent on the previous level for food, the population of each level affects the other animal groups. For instance, if an ecosystem is made up of only grass, deer, and wolves, the grass are the producers, the deer eat the grass, and the wolves eat the deer. If deer are overhunted one year, the grass is given room to grow more because less of it is consumed, but the wolves will not have enough food, so the population will reduce size. Eventually, because of the abundance of grass and a reduced population of wolves, the deer may then have a surge of population. This example is an over-simplistic example, as there are usually many more producers, consumers, and predators within an ecosystem.

Food Web in a Pond

Sunlight allows green algae to photosynthesize and grow. The algae are fed upon by small animals like water fleas and copepods. In turn, these are eaten by small worms, mosquito larvae and other larval insects. These are then eaten by mosquito fish, which in turn are eaten by larger fishes like bluegills. The bluegills are preyed upon by even larger fishes like bass and by herons, egrets and raccoons (which also eat the bass). Then the animal waste and everything that dies and settles to the bottom is decomposed by bacteria and fungi.

Food Web in a Meadow

Sunlight allows grass and other plants to grow. These plants are eaten by a variety of *herbivores* like insects, rodents, and rabbits. Their seeds are consumed by various birds such as sparrows and quail. The insects are eaten by *carnivores*, including other kinds of birds, shrews, and bats. The rodents, rabbits, and some of the birds are then eaten by larger carnivores like weasels and foxes. Also, the quail, mice, rabbits and shrews are eaten by owls at night and by hawks during the day.

Relationships Between Organisms

Organisms can interact with one another in many ways. For example, **herbivores** eat plants, and **predators**, or **carnivores**, eat other animals, or **prey**. Organisms can also **compete** for biotic or abiotic resources in an ecosystem. In addition, organisms can rely on each other through **mutualism**, which is a relationship between at least two organisms in which both organisms benefit from each other. One organism can also rely on another through **commensalism**, which is a relationship between at least two organisms in which one organism benefits while the other is not harmed or benefitted. **Parasitism** is a relationship between two organisms in which one organism is the parasite, and the other organism is the host. The parasite benefits from the relationship because the parasite obtains its nutrition from the host. The host is harmed from the relationship because the parasite is using the host's energy and giving nothing in return.

Competition

In order to survive, organisms must **compete** for resources. Competition can occur either between individuals of the same species **(intraspecific competition)** or individuals of different species **(interspecific competition)**. Each species in an ecosystem occupies a specific **niche** or role due to its unique interactions with the resources and other organisms in the ecosystem. Two species with the exact same niche cannot coexist in the same habitat because one species will **outcompete** the other, driving the other to extinction. However, niches of two species in the same habitat may partly overlap due to similar behavior, such as hunting the same prey. These species will compete more for resources, but, since they don't have exactly the same niche, they may be able to coexist. While this type of competition occurs naturally in ecosystems, competition also occurs when new species are introduced to an ecosystem. **Invasive species** are non-native, introduced species that threaten the balance of the ecosystem they have joined. Because they evolved in a different environment, invasive species can outcompete the native species in an ecosystem, leading to reductions in population numbers or extinction and other harmful outcomes in the ecosystem.

EXAMPLE

Two lizard species live in the same desert and require similar resources. They both hunt insects, rely on limited water sources, and seek shade to regulate their body temperature. Which of these relationships is most likely to occur between the two lizard species?

a. The two species will form a mutualistic relationship and hunt together.
b. The two species will not affect one another.
c. The two species will compete for limited resources such as water.
d. One species will become a predator to the other.

Choice A proposes a mutualistic relationship, where two species help one another, in this case by hunting together. Two species with similar niches are unlikely to develop a mutualistic relationship, and hunting together would not be very beneficial for either species. Choice A is probably incorrect.

Choice B proposes that the two species will not affect one another at all. This is unlikely because the two lizards occupy similar niches and require similar resources, meaning they might have to compete for limited resources. Choice B is probably incorrect.

Choice C proposes that the two species will have to compete for limited resources such as water. Species that require similar resources such as these lizard species are very likely to compete, particularly if resources ar e scarce. Choice C could be the correct answer.

Choice D proposes that one species will become a predator to the other. While some lizards do eat smaller lizard species, there is no evidence to suggest this adaptation will happen. Based on the lizard's similar diet and ecological requirements, it is more likely that they would compete for limited resources. Choice D is not the answer.

Choice C is the correct answer. Species that occupy similar niches or require the same resources, such as these two lizard species, are very likely to compete with one another.

Organisms and Environmental Changes

Sudden environmental changes can include **natural disasters**, **diseases**, and **habitat destruction**. Examples of more **gradual** changes include **climate change** or **gradual habitat loss** due to population growth, agriculture, or the harvesting of natural resources. Both sudden and gradual environmental changes have the potential to significantly disrupt the balance of an ecosystem. When organisms die due to natural disasters, disease, or environmental changes, the number of individuals in a population changes. In more sudden environmental changes, these shifts in population numbers are more dramatic. Additionally, these changes in population numbers can have a **domino effect** on the ecosystem. For example, when a predator population decreases, the prey populations increase because of the reduced risk of being hunted. However, another predator population could increase because there is now reduced **competition** for resources. Environmental changes can also affect populations by influencing the presence of certain physical traits. Because individuals with certain traits are more likely to survive specific environmental changes, those traits will become more common in a population through the process of **natural selection.**

EXAMPLE

A remote island consisting of rainforest habitats has experienced consistently rising temperatures over the course of a decade. Scientists have made several observations of changes to local populations. Which of the following observations is most likely a beneficial change to a trait that will affect subsequent generations?

a. The population of frogs has declined.
b. Old-growth trees are producing fewer leaves.
c. Birds spend less time in the canopy.
d. A small mammal species produces a thinner coat of fur.

Choice A describes a decline in the population of frogs. Rising temperatures are likely to cause certain populations to decline, particularly amphibians. However, the question asks for an example of a beneficial change to a trait that will be inherited by subsequent populations. In this case, population decline is not a change to a trait, and population decline is rarely beneficial. Choice A is not the answer.

Choice B describes trees producing fewer leaves. This answer specifies that the trees are old-growth trees, meaning they have been around for a long time. In this case, producing fewer leaves is likely to be an individual response to limited resources and environmental changes. This is unlikely to be a beneficial change because fewer leaves mean the trees cannot photosynthesize as much. In addition, this describes an immediate survival response rather than an inherited change to a trait. Choice B is probably not the answer.

Choice C describes a change in birds' behavior, who begin to spend less time in the canopy, likely to avoid the sun. Because this is a change in behavior, it is unclear whether it would be passed on to subsequent generations. Choice C is probably not the answer.

Choice D describes a change to a physical trait, specifically fur thickness in small mammal species. With rising temperatures, having thinner fur is likely to be beneficial in keeping the animal from overheating. Additionally, a physical trait is more likely to be passed on to subsequent generations than a behavioral change. Choice D is the correct answer.

Choice D is the correct answer because it describes a change to a trait that is most likely to be beneficial and to be inherited by subsequent generations.

HUMAN IMPACT ON MARINE ENVIRONMENTS

Humans can impact ecosystems directly and indirectly. For example, humans can **directly** impact an ecosystem through deforestation and overfishing, while humans can **indirectly** impact ecosystems through the burning of fossil fuels, which can contribute to climate change and pollution. Marine ecosystems are some of the most vulnerable to these impacts. For example, the ocean absorbs some of the carbon dioxide (CO_2) that goes into the atmosphere, and so as more CO_2 goes into the atmosphere due to human activity, more CO_2 goes into the ocean. This absorption has caused chemical reactions that have led the oceans to become more acidic. This **ocean acidification** poses a threat to shell-building organisms and coral. Because coral reefs provide food and habitats for a significant portion of marine life, ocean acidification poses intense danger for marine ecosystems. Human agricultural activity also contributes to ocean pollution, as **runoff** from fertilizers and other chemicals leaks into the ocean.

Overfishing and Artificial Reefs

Reliance on oceans for food has led to **overfishing**, which is when fish are caught and removed from a body of water at a higher rate than the fish can reproduce and replenish. This threatens fish populations as well as entire marine ecosystems. To increase fish populations in a certain area, humans have used **artificial reefs**, which are created by submerging materials into the water to replicate a coral reef habitat. Although artificial reefs can quickly increase the populations of fish and other marine life, they can have negative impacts, such as contributing to ocean pollution. Ironically, they can increase the fish population so much that many people will fish there and repeat the process of overfishing. Because of this, overfishing is a cyclical process that must constantly be kept in check.

Ecological Succession

Environmental changes such as natural disasters can affect whole ecosystems and individual populations. Some examples of natural disasters include forest fires, droughts, floods, earthquakes, or volcanic eruptions. When a natural disaster occurs, it threatens the balance of an ecosystem. For example, a forest fire will reduce edible vegetation and available shade from trees. A drought reduces access to water sources and affects food availability. The short-term effects of a natural disaster include a reduction in the number of individuals in a population. These population changes can lead to an effect called **ecological succession**. As some populations die or weaken due to the disaster, they leave room for other populations to thrive. These populations are called **early successional species**. Gradually, the ecosystem continues to change, eventually returning to its original state as populations increase and overtake early successional species.

Biodiversity

Biodiversity refers to the variability and variety of living things on Earth. While there are many ways to measure diversity, the most common types are species diversity and genetic variability. **Species diversity** refers to the number of species within an ecosystem or community, while **genetic variability** describes the presence of different genetic traits within a population or species. Biodiversity helps an ecosystem adapt to environmental changes and prevent collapse. When an event such as a natural disaster or human disturbance occurs, the balance of an ecosystem is affected. For example, food or water resources could become scarce, which will make it difficult for many organisms to survive. Populations with high genetic diversity will have a range of different physical traits, such as beak size or fur thickness. Some of these traits can help an organism survive by leading it to eat a more varied diet or survive cold winters, for example. These adaptive traits make it more likely that some individuals within a population will survive. Similarly, species diversity in an ecosystem increases the likelihood that some populations in an ecosystem will withstand an environmental change. In this way, biodiversity contributes to a functioning ecosystem by making ecosystems more resilient to environmental changes and threats.

Adaptation to Environment

Organisms must be able to adapt to their environment in order to thrive or survive. Individuals must be able to recognize stimuli in their surroundings and adapt quickly. For example, an individual euglena can sense light and respond by moving toward the light. Individual organisms must also be able to adapt to changes in the environment on a larger scale. For example, plants must be able to respond to the change in the length of the day to flower at the correct time. Populations must also be able to adapt to a changing environment. Evolution by **natural selection** is the process by which populations change over many generations to become better adapted to their environment, thus surviving longer and reproducing more successfully.

Natural and Artificial Selection

Natural selection and artificial selection are both mechanisms of evolution. **Natural selection** is a process of nature in which a population can change over generations. Every population has variations in individual heritable traits and organisms best suited for survival typically reproduce and pass on those genetic traits to offspring to increase the likelihood of them surviving. Typically, the more advantageous a trait is, the more common that trait becomes in a population. Natural selection brings about evolutionary **adaptations** and is responsible for biological diversity. Artificial selection is another mechanism of evolution. **Artificial selection** is a process brought about by humans. Artificial selection is the **selective breeding** of domesticated animals and plants such as when farmers choose animals or plants with desirable traits to reproduce. Artificial selection has led to the evolution of farm stock and crops. For example, cauliflower, broccoli, and cabbage all evolved due to artificial selection of the wild mustard plant.

Example of Natural Selection

Historical biologist Charles Darwin observed finches in the Galápagos islands for evidence of these changes. In more recent history, a drought occurred in the Galápagos, making food resources scarce. Scientists observed that individual finches with larger beaks were more able to adapt to this environmental change because they could eat different types of seeds, while birds with smaller beaks had difficulty finding food. Because the birds with larger beaks were more likely to find food, they were more likely to survive and produce offspring. Since beak size is a genetic or **inheritable** trait, more birds in the next generation were born with larger beaks, while the number of birds born with smaller beaks decreased over time. When environmental pressures favor a certain trait because it helps a species survive, it causes a change in the frequency of that trait within the population, and this process is called **natural selection**.

Evolution

Evolution is the process whereby organisms pass certain acquired traits to successive generations, affecting the attributes of later organisms and even leading to the creation of new species. Charles Darwin is the name often associated with the formulation of natural selection, a vital component of evolution as it is known today. **Natural selection** states that members of a species are not identical—due to their respective genetic make-ups, each individual will possess traits which make it stronger or weaker and more or less able to adapt. The other tenet of natural selection is that members of a species will always have to compete for scarce resources to survive. Therefore, organisms with traits which will help them survive are more likely to do so and produce offspring, passing along the "desirable" traits. Darwin suggested that this process, by creating groups of a species with increasingly different characteristics, would eventually lead to the formation of **a new species**.

Significant Events Leading to Evolution of Man

The **origination of life** is the most fundamental development in the history of life on Earth. Prokaryotic microfossils, the earliest fossils identified by paleontologists, are dated to near 3.5 billion years ago. However, the presence of large amounts of certain carbon and oxygen isotopes in sedimentary rocks dated at about 3.8 billion years ago may indicate the presence of organic material. The next significant event suggested by a drastic change in the fossil record is the huge diversification of species which occurred approximately 543 million years ago, near the end of the Precambrian eon and the beginning of the Phanerozoic. This theoretical evolutionary stage included higher-level tissue organization in multicellular organisms, the development of predator-prey relationships, and, most importantly, the development of skeletons. The final critical step toward the evolution of man is the emergence of life on land about 418 million years ago. This necessitated the evolution of structures which could breathe air, obtain and retain water on land, and support its own weight out of water.

Darwin's Contributions to the Theory of Evolution

Charles Darwin's theory of evolution by natural selection is the unifying concept in biology today. From 1831 to 1836, Darwin traveled as a naturalist on a five-year voyage on the *H.M.S. Beagle* around the tip of South America and to the Galápagos Islands. He studied finches, took copious amounts of meticulous notes, and collected thousands of plant and animal specimens. He collected 13 species of finches each with a unique bill for a distinct food source, which led him to believe, due to similarities between the finches, that the finches shared a common ancestor. The similarities and differences of fossils of extinct rodents and modern mammal fossils led him to believe that the mammals had changed over time. Darwin believed that these changes were the result of random genetic changes called mutations. He believed that mutations could be beneficial and eventually result in a different organism over time. In 1859, in his first book, *On the Origin of Species*, Darwin proposed that natural selection was the means by which adaptations would arise over time. He coined the term "natural selection" and said that it is the mechanism of evolution. Because variety exists among individuals of a species, he stated that those individuals must compete for the same limited resources. Some would die, and others would survive. According to Darwin, evolution is a slow, gradual process. In 1871, Darwin published his second book, *Descent of Man, and Selection in Relation to Sex*, in which he discussed the evolution of man.

Evidence Supporting Evolution

Molecular Evidence

Because all organisms are made up of cells, all organisms are alike on a fundamental level. Cells share similar components, which are made up of molecules. Specifically, all cells contain DNA and RNA. This should indicate that all species descended from a **common ancestor**. Humans and chimpanzees share approximately 98% of their genes in common, while humans and bacteria share approximately 7% of their genes in common suggesting that bacteria and humans are not closely related. Biologists have been able to use DNA sequence comparisons of modern organisms to reconstruct the "root" of the tree of life. The fact that RNA can store information, replicate itself, and code for proteins suggests that RNA could have could have evolved first, followed by DNA.

Homology

Homology is the similarity of structures of different species based on a similar anatomy in a common evolutionary ancestor. For instance, the forelimbs of humans, dogs, birds, and whales all have the same basic pattern of the bones. Specifically, all of these organisms have a humerus, radius, and ulna. They are all modifications of the same basic evolutionary structure from a common ancestor. Tetrapods resemble the fossils of extinct transitional animal called the *Eusthenopteron*. This would seem to indicate that evolution primarily modifies preexisting structures.

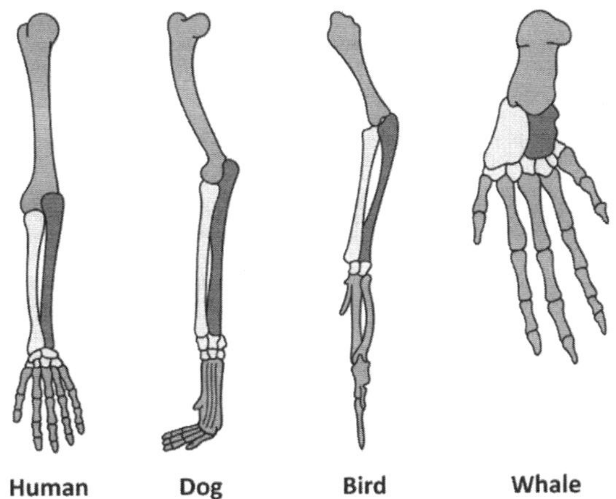

Review Video: Homologous vs Analogous Structures
Visit mometrix.com/academy and enter code: 355157

EMBRYOLOGY

The stages of **embryonic development** reveal homologies between species. These homologies are evidence of a **common ancestor**. For example, in chicken embryos and mammalian embryos, both include a stage in which slits and arches appear in the embryo's neck region that are strikingly similar to gill slits and gill arches in fish embryos. Adult chickens and adult mammals do not have gills, but this embryonic homology indicates that birds and mammals share a common ancestor with fish. As another example, some species of toothless whales have embryos that initially develop teeth that are later absorbed, which indicates that these whales have an ancestor with teeth in the adult form. Finally, most tetrapods have five-digit limbs, but birds have three-digit limbs in their wings. However, embryonic birds initially have five-digit limbs in their wings, which develop into a three-digit wing. Tetrapods such as reptiles, mammals, and birds all share a common ancestor with five digit limbs.

ENDOSYMBIOSIS THEORY

The endosymbiosis theory is foundational to evolution. Endosymbiosis provides the path for prokaryotes to give rise to eukaryotes. Specifically, **endosymbiosis** explains the development of the organelles of mitochondria in animals and chloroplasts in plants. This theory states that some eukaryotic organelles such as mitochondria and chloroplasts originated as free living cells. According to this theory, primitive, heterotrophic eukaryotes engulfed smaller, autotrophic bacteria prokaryotes, but the bacteria were not digested. Instead, the eukaryotes and the bacteria formed a symbiotic relationship. Eventually, the bacteria transformed into mitochondrion or chloroplasts.

SUPPORTING EVIDENCE

Several facts support the endosymbiosis theory. Mitochondria and chloroplasts contain their own DNA and can both only arise from other preexisting mitochondria and chloroplasts. The genomes of mitochondria and chloroplasts consist of single, circular DNA molecules with no histones. This is similar to bacteria genomes, not eukaryote genomes. Also, the RNA, ribosomes, and protein synthesis of mitochondria and chloroplasts are remarkably similar to those of bacteria, and both use oxygen to produce ATP. These organelles have a double phospholipid layer that is typical of engulfed bacteria. This theory also involves a secondary endosymbiosis in which the original eukaryotic cells that have engulfed the bacteria are then engulfed themselves by another free-living eukaryote.

Convergent Evolution

Convergent evolution is the evolutionary process in which two or more unrelated species become increasingly similar in appearance. In convergent evolution, similar adaptations in these unrelated species occur due to these species inhabiting the same kind of environment. For example, the mammals shown below, although found in different parts of the world, developed similar appearances due to their similar environments.

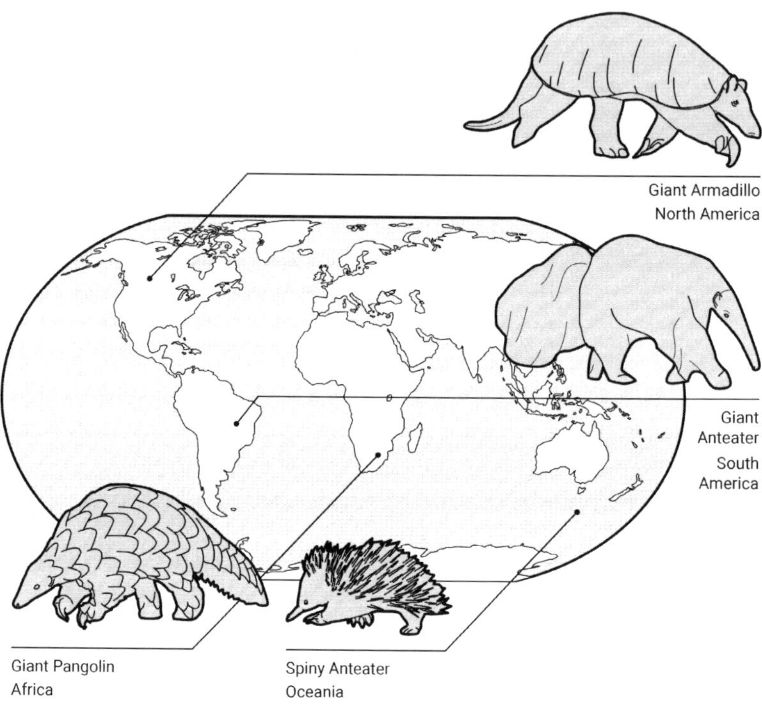

Divergent Evolution

Divergent evolution is the evolutionary process in which organisms of one species become increasingly dissimilar in appearance. As several small adaptations occur due to natural selection, the organisms will finally reach a point at which two new species are formed, also known as **speciation**. Then, these two species will further diverge from each other as they continue to evolve. Adaptive radiation is an example of divergent evolution. Another example is the divergent evolution of the wooly mammoth and the modern elephant from a common ancestor.

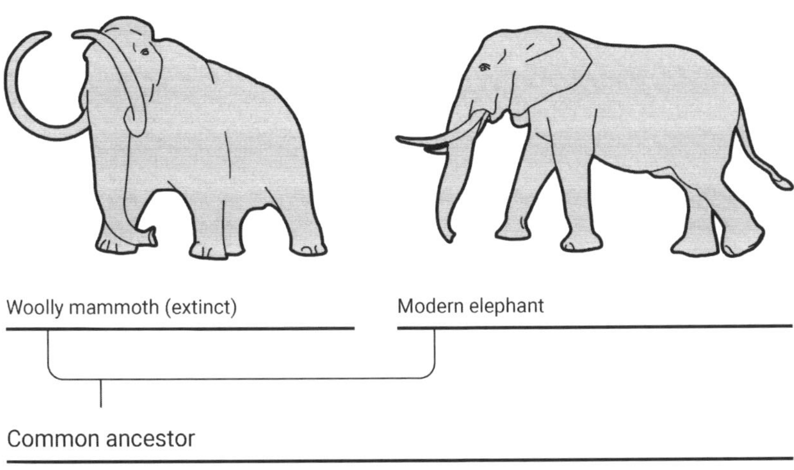

Fossil Record

The **fossil record** provides many types of support for evolution including comparisons from rock layers, transition fossils, and homologies with modern organisms. First, fossils from rock layers from all over the world have been compared, enabling scientists to develop a sequence of life from simple to complex. Based on the fossil record, the **geologic timeline** chronicles the history of all living things. For example, the fossil record clearly indicates that invertebrates developed before vertebrates and that fish developed before amphibians. Second, numerous transitional fossils have been found. **Transitional fossils** show an intermediate state between an ancestral form of an organism and the form of its descendants. These fossils show the path of evolutionary change. For example, many transition fossils documenting the evolutionary change from fish to amphibians have been discovered. In 2004, scientists discovered *Tiktaalik roseae*, or the "fishapod," which is a 375-million-year-old fossil that exhibits both fish and amphibian characteristics. Another example would be *Pakicetus*, an extinct land mammal, that scientists determined is an early ancestor of modern whales and dolphins based on the specialized structures of the inner ear. Most fossils exhibit homologies with modern organisms. For example, extinct horses are similar to modern horses, indicating a common ancestor.

Viruses

Viruses are nonliving, infectious particles that act as parasites in living organisms. Viruses are acellular, which means that they lack cell structure. Viruses cannot reproduce outside of living cells. The structure of a virus is a nucleic acid genome, which may be either DNA or RNA, surrounded by a protective protein coat or **capsid**. In some viruses, the capsid may be surrounded by a lipid membrane or envelope. Viruses can contain up to 500 genes and have various shapes. They usually are too small to be seen without the aid of an electron microscope. Viruses can infect plants, animals, fungi, protists, and bacteria. Viruses can attack only specific types of cells that have specific receptors on their surfaces. Viruses do not divide or reproduce like living cells. Instead, they use the host cell they infect by "reprogramming" it, using the nucleic acid genome, to make more copies of the virus. The host cell usually bursts to release these copies.

Bacteria

Bacteria are small, prokaryotic, single-celled organisms. Bacteria have a circular loop of DNA (plasmid) that is not contained within a nuclear membrane. Bacterial ribosomes are not bound to the endoplasmic reticulum, as in eukaryotes. A cell wall containing peptidoglycan surrounds the bacterial plasma membrane. Some bacteria such as pathogens are further encased in a gel-like, sticky layer called the **capsule**, which enhances their ability to cause disease. Bacteria can be autotrophs or heterotrophs. Some bacterial heterotrophs are saprophytes that function as decomposers in ecosystems. Many types of bacteria share commensal or mutualistic relationships with other organisms. Most bacteria reproduce asexually by binary fission. Two identical daughter cells are produced from one parent cell. Some bacteria can transfer genetic material to other bacteria through a process called conjugation, while some bacteria can incorporate DNA from the environment in a process called transformation.

Protists

Protists are small, eukaryotic, single-celled organisms. Although protists are small, they are much larger than prokaryotic bacteria. Protists have three general forms, which include plantlike protists, animal-like protists, and fungus-like protists. **Plantlike protists** are algae that contain chlorophyll and perform photosynthesis. Animal-like protists are **protozoa** with no cell walls that typically lack chlorophyll and are grouped by their method of locomotion, which may use flagella, cilia, or a different structure. **Fungus-like protists**, which do not have chitin in their cell walls, are generally grouped as either slime molds or water molds. Protists may be autotrophic or heterotrophic. Autotrophic protists include many species of algae, while heterotrophic protists include parasitic, commensal, and mutualistic protozoa. Slime molds are heterotrophic fungus-like protists, which consume microorganisms. Some protists reproduce sexually, but most reproduce asexually by binary fission. Some reproduce asexually by spores while others reproduce by alternation of generations and require two hosts in their life cycle.

Fungi

Fungi are nonmotile organisms with eukaryotic cells and contain chitin in their cell walls. Most fungi are multicellular, but a few including yeast are unicellular. Fungi have multicellular filaments called **hyphae** that are grouped together into the mycelium. Fungi do not perform photosynthesis and are considered heterotrophs. Fungi can be parasitic, mutualistic or free living. Free-living fungi include mushrooms and toadstools. Parasitic fungi include fungi responsible for ringworm and athlete's foot. Mycorrhizae are mutualistic fungi that live in or near plant roots increasing the roots' surface area of absorption. Almost all fungi reproduce asexually by spores, but most fungi also have a sexual phase in the production of spores. Some fungi reproduce by budding or fragmentation.

> **Review Video: Feeding Among Heterotrophs**
> Visit mometrix.com/academy and enter code: 836017

PARASITES

Parasites are organisms that live on or inside another organism called a *host*. The parasite drains energy from the host and may release substances that harm it. Many parasites cause the host to get sick and eventually may even kill it. However, with parasites the host is not killed outright as with predation. Certain kinds of worms, mosquitoes, and ticks are examples of parasites.

Epidemic and Pandemics

Epidemics are usually confined to a specific population or region. **Pandemics**, however, are wide spread throughout multiple countries or the whole world. Because of the rapid increase in international marketing and travel, it is now almost impossible to completely contain an outbreak that at one time may have been local, such as Ebola (which has killed over 11,000 people), HIV (which has killed over 35 million people), and most recently, the COVID-19, killing half a million Americans in its first year. Additionally, health laws and practices vary widely, so not all populations have adequate preventive care or treatment. Thus, any outbreak can pose a worldwide threat. Viruses, especially, pose a grave threat because they readily mutate and treatment may be unavailable or inadequate.

Plants

Plants are multicellular organisms with eukaryotic cells containing cellulose in their cell walls. Plant cells have chlorophyll and perform photosynthesis. Plants can be vascular or nonvascular. **Vascular plants** have true leaves, stems, and roots that contain xylem and phloem. **Nonvascular plants** lack true leaves, stems and roots and do not have any true vascular tissue but instead rely on diffusion and osmosis to transport most of materials or resources needed to survive. Almost all plants are autotrophic, relying on photosynthesis for food. A small number do not have chlorophyll and are parasitic, but these are extremely rare. Plants can reproduce sexually or asexually. Many plants reproduce by seeds produced in the fruits of the plants, while some plants reproduce by seeds on cones. One type of plant, ferns, reproduce by a different system that utilizes spores. Some plants can even reproduce asexually by vegetative reproduction.

> **Review Video: Kingdom Plantae**
> Visit mometrix.com/academy and enter code: 710084

MAJOR PLANT PROCESSES

There are three key processes that plants need to survive: photosynthesis, respiration, and transpiration. **Photosynthesis** is the process that plants use to create food. Photosynthesis requires water, carbon dioxide, and sunlight. Photosynthesis creates glucose molecules that can be broken down and used as energy for the plant. The cellular **respiration** process breaks glucose molecules into usable energy for the cell. Respiration requires oxygen to take place, so the plants take in oxygen. **Transpiration** is the process of plants losing water through their leaves. Plants can control the amount of water lost through their leaves. Water is lost through stomata on the underside of the leaves. Stomata can be opened and closed by guard cells.

NET EQUATION FOR PHOTOSYNTHESIS

Photosynthesis is the food-making process in green plants. Photosynthesis occurs in the chloroplasts of cells in the presence of light and chlorophyll. The reactants are **carbon dioxide** and **water**. The energy from the sunlight is absorbed and stored in the glucose molecules. The net equation for photosynthesis can be represented by the following equations:

$$\text{carbon dioxide} + \text{water} + \text{light} \xrightarrow{\text{chlorophyll}} \text{glucose} + \text{oxygen}$$

$$6CO_2 + 6H_2O + \text{light} \xrightarrow{\text{chlorophyll}} C_6H_{12}O_6 + 6O_2$$

The products of photosynthesis are glucose and oxygen gas.

RESPIRATION

Cellular respiration is the process in which energy is released from glucose in the form of adenosine triphosphate (ATP). **Cellular respiration** is the reverse process of photosynthesis. In cellular respiration, glucose is burned or combined with oxygen as shown in the following equations:

$$\text{glucose} + \text{oxygen} \rightarrow \text{carbon dioxide} + \text{water} + \text{ATP}$$

$$C_6H_{12}O_6 + 6O_2 \rightarrow 6CO_2 + 6H_2O$$

The products of cellular respiration are carbon dioxide and water. Energy is released from glucose in the form of ATP.

TRANSPIRATION

Transpiration is the mechanism by which water evaporates into the atmosphere from the leaves or stems of plants. Plants absorb water into their roots through osmosis. Then, as explained by **cohesion-tension theory**, water moves upward from the roots of a plant to its leaves. Some transpiration occurs directly through surface cells on the stem of a plant. More often, however, water escapes through pores in its leaves called **stomates**. Water droplets on the exterior surface of the leaves (usually on the bottom of the leaves) are consequently subjected to the process of evaporation. The process of transpiration enables **photosynthesis**, which in turn releases vital oxygen into Earth's atmosphere. Transpiration also has a cooling effect on the surface and air around the plant.

Carbon Cycle

Carbon drives photosynthesis; is a major component in nutrients such as fat, protein and carbohydrates; and provides energy in the form of hydrocarbons. All of these characteristics make it imperative to understanding the **carbon cycle**. Carbon is involved in a multitude of processes and steadily moves through the carbon cycle. In the atmosphere, carbon attaches to oxygen to create carbon dioxide. Plants breathe in carbon dioxide and use it during photosynthesis to create a carbon-containing molecule called glucose. The carbon becomes part of the plant. Animals consume the plant, consuming the carbon. Dead organisms and waste materials containing carbon decompose and become part of the soil, eventually creating carbon-containing fossil fuels. When we burn fossil fuels, carbon is released into the atmosphere. Carbon is also released into the atmosphere by animal respiration, plant respiration, and even root respiration.

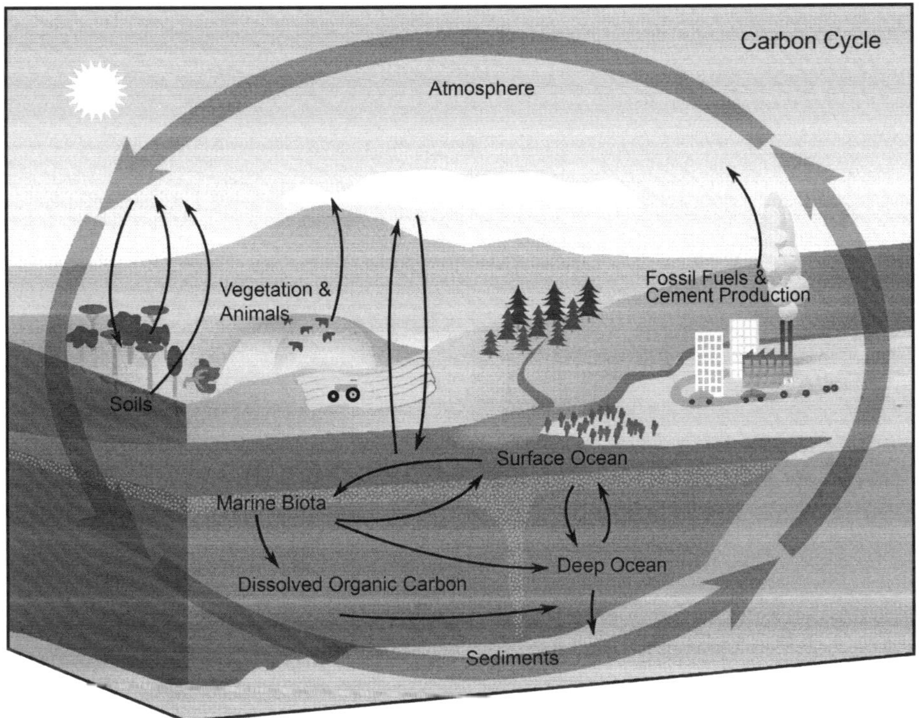

Earth and Space Science

Properties That Contribute to Earth's Life-Sustaining System

Life on earth is dependent on:

- All three states of **water** – gas (water vapor), liquid, and solid (ice)
- A variety of forms of **carbon**, the basis of life (carbon-based units)
- In the atmosphere, carbon dioxide, in the forms of methane and black carbon soot, produces the **greenhouse effect** that provides a habitable atmosphere.
- The earth's **atmosphere and electromagnetic field**, which shield the surface from harmful radiation and allow useful radiation to go through.
- The **earth's relationship to the sun and the moon**, which creates the four seasons and the cycles of plant and animal life.
- The combination of **water, carbon, and nutrients** that provides sustenance for life and regulates the climate system in a habitable temperature range with non-toxic air.

Hydrosphere and Hydrologic Cycle

The **hydrosphere** is anything on Earth that is related to water, whether it is in the air, on land, or in a plant or animal system. A water molecule consists of only two atoms of hydrogen and one of oxygen, yet it is what makes life possible. Unlike any other planets that have been discovered, Earth is able to sustain water in a liquid state most of the time. Water vapor and ice are of no use to living organisms. The **hydrologic cycle** is the journey water takes as it proceeds through different forms. Liquid surface water evaporates to form the gaseous state of a cloud, and then becomes liquid again in the form of rain. This process takes about 10 days. This cycle is for surface water only: rivers, lakes, groundwater, ocean surface, etc. Water in the deep ocean and in the heart of glaciers is typically sequestered from the cycle for many thousands of years.

Water Cycle

The **water cycle** refers to the circulation of water in the Earth's hydrosphere (below the surface, on the surface, and above the surface of the Earth). This continuous process involves five physical actions.

- **Evaporation** refers to liquid water heating up and changing to into a gas, known as water vapor.
- **Transpiration** is where water inside of plants evaporates directly out of plant leaves.
- **Condensation** refers to the water vapor cooling down and beginning to turn back into a liquid form, causing clouds to form.
- **Precipitation** refers to the rain, snow, hail, or sleet that falls from clouds once the water vapor has condensed enough.

- The **storage** stage of the water cycle refers to the water being stored in the ground, trees, or bodies of water on the earth. Water is either trapped in vegetation (interception) or absorbed into the surface (infiltration). Runoff, caused by gravity, physically moves water downward into oceans or other water bodies.

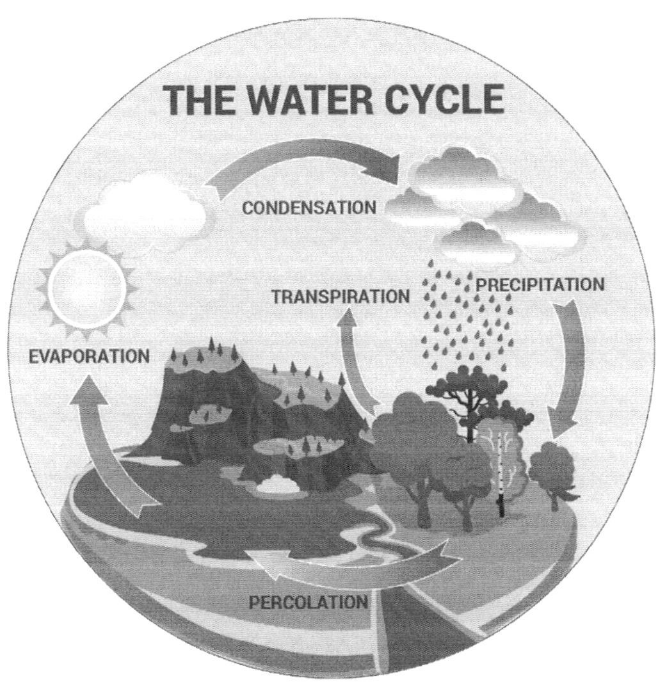

Review Video: Hydrologic Cycle
Visit mometrix.com/academy and enter code: 426578

Oceans, Seas, Lakes, Rivers, and Canals

- **Oceans** are the largest bodies of water on earth and cover nearly 71% of the earth's surface. There are five major oceans: Atlantic, Pacific (largest and deepest), Indian, Arctic, and Southern (surrounds Antarctica). The deepest part of the ocean is approximately 11,000 meters below sea level.
- **Seas** are smaller than oceans and are somewhat surrounded by land like a lake, but lakes are fresh water and seas are salt water. Seas include the Mediterranean, Baltic, Caspian, Caribbean, and Coral.
- **Lakes** are bodies of water in a depression on the earth's surface. Examples of lakes are the Great Lakes and Lake Victoria.
- **Rivers** are a channeled flow of water that start out as a spring or stream formed by runoff from rain or snow. Rivers flow from higher to lower ground, and usually empty into a sea or ocean. Great rivers of the world include the Amazon, Nile, Rhine, Mississippi, Ganges, Mekong, and Yangtze.

Rock Cycle

The **rock cycle** is the process whereby the materials that make up the Earth transition through the three types of rock: igneous, sedimentary, and metamorphic. Rocks, like all matter, cannot be created or destroyed; rather, they undergo a series of changes and adopt different forms through the functions of the rock cycle. Plate tectonics and the water cycle are the driving forces behind the rock cycle; they force rocks and minerals out of equilibrium and force them to adjust to different external conditions. Viewed in a generalized, cyclical fashion, the rock cycle operates as follows: rocks beneath Earth's surface melt into magma. This **magma** either erupts through volcanoes or remains inside the Earth. Regardless, the magma cools, forming igneous rocks. On the surface, these rocks experience **weathering** and **erosion**, which break them down and distribute the fragments across the surface. These fragments form layers and eventually become **sedimentary rocks**. Sedimentary rocks are then either transformed to **metamorphic rocks** (which will become magma inside the Earth) or melted down into magma.

Rock Formation

Igneous Rocks: Igneous rocks can be formed from sedimentary rocks, metamorphic rocks, or other igneous rocks. Rocks that are pushed under the Earth's surface (usually due to plate subduction) are exposed to high mantle temperatures, which cause the rocks to melt into magma. The magma then rises to the surface through volcanic processes. The lower atmospheric temperature causes the magma to cool, forming grainy, extrusive igneous rocks. The creation of extrusive, or volcanic, rocks is quite rapid. The cooling process can occur so rapidly that crystals do not form; in this case, the result is a glass, such as obsidian. It is also possible for magma to cool down inside the Earth's interior; this type of igneous rock is called intrusive. Intrusive, or plutonic, rocks cool more slowly, resulting in a coarse-grained texture.

Sedimentary Rocks: Sedimentary rocks are formed when rocks at the Earth's surface experience weathering and erosion, which break them down and distribute the fragments across the surface. Fragmented material (small pieces of rock, organic debris, and the chemical products of mineral sublimation) is deposited and accumulates in layers, with top layers burying the materials beneath. The pressure exerted by the topmost layers causes the lower layers to compact, creating solid sedimentary rock in a process called lithification.

Fossil Fuels

Sedimentary rock can contain the remains of living organisms. This happens when clasts are deposited on top of remains or pieces of remains are deposited among the clasts. Over time and with pressure, these remains become substances called **fossil fuels** that can fuel machines. Some examples of fossil fuels are oil and coal.

Example

Which of the following best explains how fossil fuels are formed?

a. Fossils created from the mass extinction of dinosaurs gradually broke down into fuel such as oil.
b. Decaying plants and animals at the bottom of the ocean were compressed into fuel such as oil.
c. The remains of animals encased in ice from the last ice age melted, releasing fuel such as oil.
d. Fossils and bones are processed by humans to create fuels such as oil.

Choice A states that fossil fuels were formed from dinosaur fossils. The production of fossil fuels is unrelated to fossils, despite their name. Fossil fuels are formed from the remains of ancient plants and animals, not dinosaur fossils. Choice A is incorrect.

Choice B proposes that fossil fuels were formed from the remains of plants and animals in the ocean. Over very long periods of time, pressure and heat can turn these remains into fossil fuels. Choice B could be the correct answer.

Choice C states that fossil fuels are the result of animal remains that have become encased in ice during an ice age melting. When this happens, it typically preserves the remains of the animals, and they do not decay or transform into materials such as fossil fuels. Choice C is not the answer.

Choice D has to do with fossils being processed by humans to create fossil fuels. Fossil fuels do not actually come from fossils, and they are created through natural processes over hundreds of millions of years, not by humans. Choice D is incorrect.

Choice B is the correct answer. Fossil fuels are created not from fossils, but from decaying remains of plants and animals in the ocean due to extreme amounts of time, pressure, and heat.

Metamorphic Rocks: Metamorphic rocks are igneous or sedimentary rocks that have "morphed" into another kind of rock. In metamorphism, high temperatures and levels of pressure change preexisting rocks physically and/or chemically, which produces different species of rocks. In the rock cycle, this process generally occurs in materials that have been thrust back into the Earth's mantle by plate subduction. Regional metamorphism refers to a large band of metamorphic activity; this often occurs near areas of high orogenic (mountain-building) activity. Contact metamorphism refers to metamorphism that occurs when "country rock" (that is, rock native to an area) comes into contact with high-heat igneous intrusions (magma).

Role of Water

Water plays an important role in the rock cycle through its roles in **erosion** and **weathering**: it wears down rocks; it contributes to the dissolution of rocks and minerals as acidic soil water; and it carries ions and rock fragments (sediments) to basins where they will be compressed into **sedimentary rock**. Water also plays a role in the **metamorphic processes** that occur underwater in newly-formed igneous rock at mid-ocean ridges. The presence of water (and other volatiles) is a vital component in the melting of rocky crust into magma above subduction zones.

Review Video: Igneous, Sedimentary, and Metamorphic Rocks
Visit mometrix.com/academy and enter code: 689294

Soils

Soils are formed when rock is broken down into smaller and smaller fragments by physical, chemical, and biological processes. This is called **weathering**. *Physical processes* include **erosion** and **transportation** by water and wind, freezing and thawing, and slumping due to gravity. *Chemical changes* alter the original substances present in rocks and early-stage soils. *Biological processes* include burrowing by animals like earthworms and rodents and penetration by plant roots. As plants and animals die and **decay**, soils become rich in dark organic matter called *humus*.

Properties of Soil

Since soil is a mixture of rock fragments and biological materials, it varies significantly. The composition of soil determines whether it will be good for plant life or not. Several properties of soil can be used to identify its composition, which can be helpful for adjusting it for suitability for plant growth.

- **Texture** refers to the size of the particles, which are classified as sand, silt, or clay, depending on the size and mixture of the particles.
- **Structure** refers to the density and arrangement of the soil particles. Soil can be compacted, making it dense and rock-like or it can be loose and easy to work with when planting.
- **Porosity** refers to how well water flows through the soil. A higher sand content usually allows water to flow through the soil more easily, whereas clay tends to hold onto water.
- **Chemistry** cannot be seen, but can be tested for the actual elements present in a sample of soil.
- **Color** of soil changes based on the types of minerals and organic matter in the soil. Redder soil may indicate that there is oxidized (rusted) iron in the soil, for instance.

Mineral Properties

Minerals are important because they act as the building blocks for rocks, which create the surface of the Earth. Minerals can be identified based on their many properties, which include hardness, color, luster (or shininess), cleavage (the way a mineral breaks or splits apart), and streak color (the color left after scratching a mineral against a tile). Calcite, for example, is an important mineral that is defined by its softness, white color, dullness, block-like cleavage pattern, and white streak color. Quartz, on the other hand, is defined by is hardness, varying colors, glassy luster, fracturing (breaking into pieces that are not smooth), and white streak color. While these two minerals have some similar properties, their hardness, luster, and cleavage would help scientists know they are two different minerals.

WEATHERING

The rocks at Earth's surface experience physical, biological, and chemical processes that are much different from the processes ambient during their formations. The operation of these processes on Earth materials is called weathering.

MECHANICAL WEATHERING

Mechanical weathering causes disintegration of rocks and minerals. In this process, the affected rocks break apart into small fragments but retain their chemical compositions. This type of weathering occurs due to the presence of joints, or cracks, in rocks that allow the penetration of water and vegetative roots. Mechanical weathering occurs most often in cooler climates. The subtypes of mechanical weathering are pressure release, exfoliation, freeze-thaw, and salt-crystal growth:

- **Pressure release**, or surface unloading, occurs when erosion removes materials overlying rock. Decreased pressure causes the underlying rocks to expand and fracture.
- **Exfoliation** often occurs in regions with some moisture that experience substantial diurnal temperature changes. Rocks are subjected to heat during the day, which causes them to expand. At night, the much cooler temperatures cause the rocks to compact. The repeated expansion and contraction creates stress in the outer layers of the rocks, which eventually begin to "peel" off in thin layers. Exfoliation can also be caused by pressure release.
- **Freeze-thaw** operates when water, which has penetrated the joints of a rock, freezes and expands. The resultant pressure widens the joints and can even shatter the rock. If the rock does not fracture, the thawing of ice in the joints admits water further into the rock. Continuous, long-term freeze-thaw activity weakens rocks.
- In **salt-crystal growth**, the evaporation of saline solutions within rocks leaves salt crystals behind. Pressures accompanying this crystallization can be very high.

CHEMICAL WEATHERING

Chemical weathering refers to the processes by which rocks experience chemical changes (such as decomposition and decay) due to the influence of organic acids. Chemical weathering occurs most often in high temperature, high humidity climates. The two types of weathering are not mutually exclusive; they often occur side by side. The subtypes of chemical weathering are hydration, hydrolysis, oxidation, and solution:

- **Hydration** occurs when salt minerals, which are part of a rock, expand and change due to the absorption of water. For example, anhydrite changes to gypsum with the addition of water. Hydration can cause rocks to fragment mechanically.
- **Hydrolysis** involves a chemical reaction between acidic water and a rock-forming mineral. The interaction breaks the rock down into new materials. For instance, the chemical reaction between feldspar and acidic water produces quartz and clay.
- **Oxidation**, or rusting, which results in yellow, brown, or red discoloration, occurs in iron-bearing minerals when they are exposed to the atmosphere.
- **Solution** is the weathering process whereby an organic acid interacts with certain minerals in a rock, producing ions that are then washed away by erosion. Solution, therefore, is a gradual dissolving process. It produces underground channels and caverns.

EROSION

Erosion is a natural process whereby Earth's landforms are broken down through weathering. Rain and wind wear away solid matter. Over time, rain reduces mountains to hills. Rocks break off from mountains and, in turn, disintegrate into sand. Weathering and the resulting erosion always occur in downhill directions. Rain washes rocks off mountains and down streams. Rains, rivers, and streams wash soils away, and ocean waves break down adjacent cliffs. Rocks, dirt, and sand change their form and location through erosion. They do not simply vanish. These transformations and movements are called mass wasting, which occurs chemically (as when rock is dissolved by chemicals in water) or mechanically (as when rock is broken into pieces). Because materials travel as a result of mass wasting, erosion can both break down some areas and build up others. For example, a river runs through and erodes a mountain, carrying the resulting sediment downstream. This sediment gradually builds up, creating wetlands at the river's mouth. A good example of this process is Louisiana's swamps, which were created by sediment transported by the Mississippi River.

Layers of the Earth

The Earth has several distinct layers, each with its own properties:

- **Crust** – This is the outermost layer of the Earth that is comprised of the continents and the ocean basins. It has a variable thickness (35-70 km in the continents and 5-10 km in the ocean basins) and is composed mostly of alumino-silicates.
- **Mantle** – This is about 2900 km thick, and is made up mostly of ferro-magnesium silicates. It is divided into an upper and lower mantle. Most of the internal heat of the Earth is located in the mantle. Large convective cells circulate heat, and may cause plate tectonic movement.
- **Core** – This is separated into the liquid outer core and the solid inner core. The outer core is 2300 km thick (composed mostly of nickel-iron alloy), and the inner core (almost entirely iron) is 12 km thick. The Earth's magnetic field is thought to be controlled by the liquid outer core.

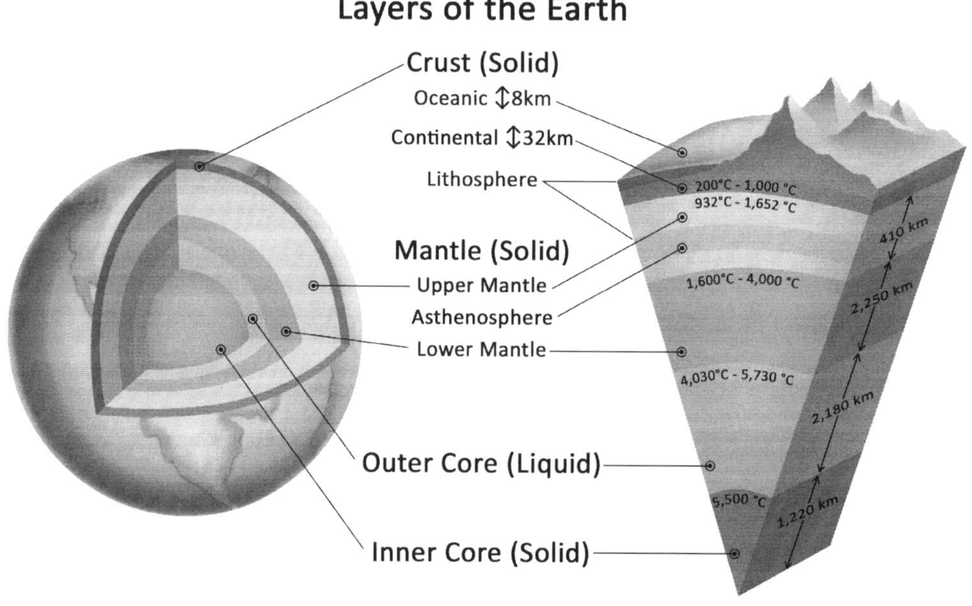

Natural Resources

The term **natural resources** refers to products and energy that can be harvested from the world and used.

- **Water** is one of the most abundant resources on the Earth and is necessary for life.
- **Natural gas** and **oil** exist underground and deep in the ocean and can be used as fuel for machines.
- **Trees** can be harvested for wood and paper and other byproducts that are used in daily life.
- **Metals** can be harvested from the ground and are used in many applications, such as building materials and in electronics.
- **Sand** can be used to make glass, soaps, and electronics.
- **Sunlight** and **wind** can be harvested with solar panels and wind turbines to generate electricity.
- **Animal products** are used for food or materials in clothing and some manufacturing processes.

Renewable and Non-renewable Resources

Materials and energy on the Earth are classified as either renewable or non-renewable. The term **renewable resources** refers to resources that are not going to run out due to overuse or can be easily reclaimed once used. This includes the sun, wind, and water. Some plants and animals grow so fast that it would be very challenging to run out and cause any form of extinction. **Non-renewable resources** include materials that take a very long time to produce, such as fossil fuels and coal. Once the Earth's population uses these materials up, it is very difficult to obtain or impossible to create more. Because renewable resources do not run out, whereas non-renewable resources do, environmentalists and scientists are always looking for new renewable resources to supply the planet with energy and for ways to reduce consumption of non-renewable resources. This reduction of consumption is known as **conservation**.

Layers of the Earth

The Earth has several distinct layers, each with its own properties:

- **Crust** – This is the outermost layer of the Earth that is comprised of the continents and the ocean basins. It has a variable thickness (35-70 km in the continents and 5-10 km in the ocean basins) and is composed mostly of alumino-silicates.
- **Mantle** – This is about 2900 km thick, and is made up mostly of ferro-magnesium silicates. It is divided into an upper and lower mantle. Most of the internal heat of the Earth is located in the mantle. Large convective cells circulate heat, and may cause plate tectonic movement.
- **Core** – This is separated into the liquid outer core and the solid inner core. The outer core is 2300 km thick (composed mostly of nickel-iron alloy), and the inner core (almost entirely iron) is 12 km thick. The Earth's magnetic field is thought to be controlled by the liquid outer core.

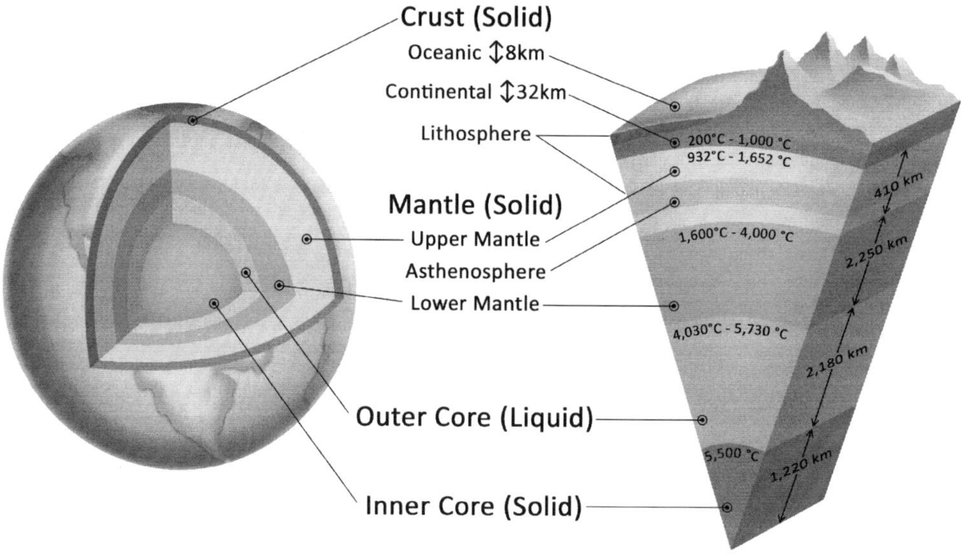

Plate Tectonics

Main Concepts

Plate tectonics is a geological theory that was developed to explain the process of continental drift. The theoretical separation of the Earth's lithosphere and asthenosphere is based upon the mechanical properties of the materials in the two respective layers and is distinct from the chemical separation of Earth's crust, mantle, and core. The lithosphere is the solid outer section of the earth. This includes the crust and the upper portion of the upper mantle. The asthenosphere, which lies in the upper mantle, is below the lithosphere. According to the theory of plate tectonics, the Earth's lithosphere is divided into **ten major plates**: African, Antarctic, Australian, Eurasian, North American, South American, Pacific, Cocos, Nazca, and Indian; it floats atop the asthenosphere. The plates of the lithosphere abut one another at plate boundaries (divergent, convergent, or transform fault), where the formation of topological features of Earth's surface begins.

Seafloor Spreading

Seafloor spreading was originally put forth as an explanation for the existence of midocean ridges such as the Mid-Atlantic Ridge. These ridges were identified as features of a vast undersea mountain system that spans the globe. Seafloor spreading postulates that the ocean floor expands outward from these ridges. The process occurs when the upper mantle layer of the Earth (the asthenosphere), just beneath the planet's crust, is heated through convection. The heat causes the asthenosphere to become more elastic and less dense. This heated material causes the crust to bow outward and eventually separate. The lighter material then flows out through the resultant rift and hardens, forming new oceanic crust. If a rift opens completely into an ocean, the basin will be flooded with seawater and create a new sea. Often, the process results in failed rifts, rifts that stopped opening before complete separation is achieved.

Continental Drift

Continental drift is a theory that explains the separation and movement of the continents based on shifts in a plastic layer of Earth's interior caused by the planet's rotation (seafloor spreading). Continental drift is part of the larger theory of plate tectonics. In the early twentieth century, many scientists and scholars noted that the edges of certain continents seemed to look like connecting pieces of a puzzle. Due to this observation, as well as the fact that similar geologic features, fossils, fauna, and flora existed on the Atlantic coasts of continents like South America and Africa, these observers theorized the previous existence of a supercontinent (referred to as Pangaea), in which all of the discrete continents identifiable today were joined together.

Theory

This theory of plate tectonics arose from the fusion of **continental drift** (first proposed in 1915 by Alfred Wegener) and **seafloor spreading** (first observed by Icelandic fishermen in the 1800s and later refined by Harry Hess and Robert Dietz in the early 1960s) in the late 1960s and early 1970s. Prior to this time, the generally accepted explanation for continental drift was that the continents were floating on the Earth's oceans. The discovery that mountains have "roots" (proved by George Airy in the early 1950s) did not categorically disprove the concept of floating continents; scientists were still uncertain as to where those mountainous roots were attached. It was not until the identification and study of the Mid-Atlantic Ridge and magnetic striping in the 1960s that plate tectonics became accepted as a scientific theory. Its conception was a landmark event in the field of Earth sciences—it provided an explanation for the empirical observations of continental drift and seafloor spreading.

Tectonic Plate Motion

The two main sources of **tectonic plate motion** are **gravity** and **friction**. The energy driving tectonic plate motion comes from the dissipation of heat from the mantle in the relatively weak asthenosphere. This energy is converted into gravity or friction to incite the motion of plates. Gravity is subdivided by geologists into ridge-push and slab-pull. In the phenomenon of **ridge-push**, the motion of plates is instigated by the energy that causes low-density material from the mantle to rise at an oceanic ridge. This leads to the situation of certain plates at higher elevations; gravity causes material to slide downhill. In **slab-pull**, plate motion is thought to be caused by cold, heavy plates at oceanic trenches sinking back into the mantle, providing fuel for future convection. Friction is subdivided into mantle drag and trench suction. Mantle drag suggests that plates move due to the friction between the lithosphere and the asthenosphere. Trench suction involves a downward frictional pull on oceanic plates in subduction zones due to convection currents.

Review Video: Plate Tectonic Theory
Visit mometrix.com/academy and enter code: 535013

Results of Tectonic Plate Motion

Earthquakes result from the movement of a dozen or so major lithospheric (crustal) plates that float upon Earth's mantle (asthenosphere). These **plates** move about each other, at **transform boundaries**, in response to complex convection cells set in motion by Earth's interior heat. Two plates move apart from each other at **divergent boundaries**, or spreading centers, and come together at **convergent boundaries**. When thin, denser, iron- and magnesium- rich oceanic crust collides with thicker, lighter, silica-rich continental crust, the former is **subducted** beneath the latter. The subducted material carries scraped-off continental crust and seawater down with it. As this material melts, it rises as a mixture of magma and steam to produce explosive **volcanic mountain ranges** such as those surrounding the Pacific Ocean Basin. A **hot spot** is an area of the Earth's surface that experiences high levels of volcanic activity, created by hypothetical phenomena called mantle plumes. Mantle plumes are exceptionally hot portions of the Earth's mantle that rise (through convection) to the crust. Hot spots are responsible for the formation of volcanic chains such as the Hawaiian Islands. When two continental plates collide at convergent boundaries, the crust buckles and thrusts up massive mountain ranges such as the Alps and Himalayas.

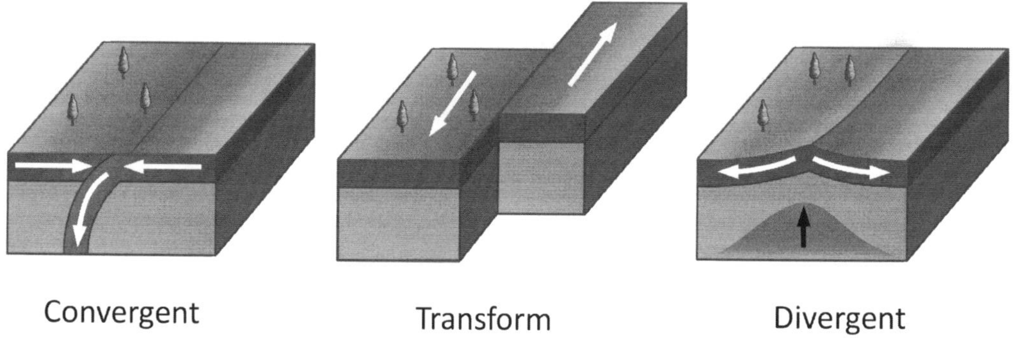

Example

The Andes volcanic mountain range on the western coast of South America is the longest mountain range in the world, consisting of hundreds of volcanoes. Which of the following processes is most likely responsible for the formation of these volcanoes?

a. Convergence of a continental plate and oceanic plate
b. Two tectonic plates moving side-by-side
c. Divergence of two tectonic plates
d. Existence of a hotspot

Choice A describes a continental plate, also referred to as a land plate, colliding with an oceanic plate. When this happens, the oceanic plate slides underneath the continental plate, which is called subduction. This results in long chains of volcanoes, such as the Cascades in the United States, along with earthquakes and sometimes tsunamis. The Andes are a long chain of volcanoes, so Choice A could be correct.

Choice B describes two tectonic plates moving side-by-side. When this happens, it causes earthquakes and rolling hills, not volcanoes. Choice B is not the answer.

Choice C describes the divergence, or separation, of two continental plates. This results in large troughs in the land called rift valleys, not volcanoes. Choice C is not the answer.

Choice D describes the existence of a hotspot, which is a high-temperature spot below Earth's crust that causes magma to rise up through the crust. Hotspots form individual volcanoes or small volcanic groups, such as those in Hawaii and Yellowstone. However, the Andes are a long chain of volcanic mountains, which are not associated with hotspots. Choice D is incorrect.

Choice A is the correct answer. Chains of volcanic mountains like the Andes are formed through subduction when an oceanic plate slides underneath a continental plate.

Determining the Order in Which Geologic Events Occurred Using the Rock Record

The **Law of Superposition** logically assumes that the bottom layer of a series of sedimentary layers is the oldest, unless it has been overturned or older rock has been pushed over it. In addition, igneous intrusions can cut through or flow above already present rocks (e.g., lava flows). This is a further indication that the lower rock layers are older. Another guideline for the rock record is that **rock layers** are older than the folds and faults in them because the rocks must exist before they can be folded or faulted. If a rock contains **atomic nuclei**, reference tables of the half-lives of commonly used radio isotopes can be used to match the decay rate of known substances to the nuclei in a rock, and thereby determine its age. Ages of rocks can also be determined from **contact metamorphism**, the re-crystallization of pre-existing rocks due to changes in physical and chemical conditions, such as heat, pressure, and chemically active fluids that might be present in lava or polluted waters.

Matching Rocks and Geologic Events in One Place with Those of Another

Geologists physically follow rock layers from one location to another by a process called "walking the outcrop." Geologists walk along the outcropping to see where it goes and what the differences and similarities of the neighboring locations they cross are. Similar rock **types** or **patterns** of rock layers that are similar in terms of thickness, color, composition, and fossil remains tell geologists that two locations have a similar geologic history. Fossils are found all over the Earth, but are from a relatively **small time period** in Earth's history. Therefore, fossil evidence helps date a rock layer, regardless of where it occurs. **Volcanic ash** is a good time indicator since ash is deposited quickly over a widespread area. Matching the date of an eruption to the ash allows for a precise identification of time. Similarly, the **meteor impact** at the intersection of the Cretaceous and Tertiary Periods left a time marker. Wherever the meteor's iridium content is found, geologists are able to date rock layers.

Sequencing the Earth's Geologic History from the Fossil and Rock Record

Reference tables are used to match specimens and time periods. For example, the fossil record has been divided into time units of the Earth's history. Rocks can therefore be dated by the fossils found with them. There are also reference tables for dating plate motions and mountain building events in geologic history. Since humans have been around for a relatively short period of time, **fossilized human remains** help to affix a date to a location. Some areas have missing **geologic layers** because of erosion or other factors, but reference tables specific to a region will list what is complete or missing. The theory of **uniformitarianism** assumes that geologic processes have been the same throughout history. Therefore, the way erosion or volcanic eruptions happen today is the same as the way these events happened millions of years ago because there is no reason for them to have changed. Therefore, knowledge about current events can be applied to the past to make judgments about events in the rock record.

Revealing Changes in Earth's History by the Fossil and Rock Records

Fossils can show how animal and plant life have changed or remained the same over time. For example, fossils have provided evidence of the existence of dinosaurs even though they no longer roam the Earth, and have also been used to prove that certain insects have been around for hundreds of millions of years. Fossils have been used to identify four basic eras: **Proterozoic**, the age of primitive life; **Paleozoic**, the age of fishes; **Mesozoic**, the age of dinosaurs; and **Cenozoic**, the age of mammals. Most ancient forms of life have disappeared, and there are reference tables that list when this occurred. Fossil records also show the evolution of certain life forms, such as the horse from the eohippus. However, the majority of changes do not involve evolution from simple to complex forms, but rather an increase in the variety of forms.

Paleontology

Paleontology is the study of prehistoric plant and animal life through the analysis of **fossil remains**. These fossils reveal the ecologies of the past and the path of evolution for both extinct and living organisms. A historical science, paleontology seeks information about the identity, origin, environment, and evolution of past organisms and what they can reveal about the past of the Earth as a whole. Paleontologists seek to explain causes rather than conduct experiments to observe effects. It is related to the fields of biology, geology, and archaeology, and is divided into several sub-disciplines concerned with the types of fossils studied, the process of fossilization, and the ecology and climate of the past. Paleontologists also help identify the composition of the Earth's rock layers by the fossils that are found, thus identifying potential sites for oil, mineral, and water extraction.

Types of Biomes

Biomes

The biosphere consists of numerous biomes. A **biome** is a large region that supports a specific community. Each biome has a characteristic climate and geography. Differences in latitude, altitude, and worldwide patterns affect temperature, precipitation, and humidity. Biomes can be classified as terrestrial or aquatic biomes. **Terrestrial biomes** include ecosystems with land environments, such as tundra, coniferous forest, temperate broadleaf forest, temperate grassland, chaparral, desert, savannas, and tropical forests. Terrestrial biomes tend to grade into each other in regions called ecotones. **Aquatic biomes** are water-dwelling ecosystems. Aquatic biomes include areas such as lakes, rivers, estuaries, coral reefs, oceanic pelagic zone, intertidal zone, and the abyssal zone.

Aquatic Biomes

Aquatic biomes are characterized by multiple factors including the temperature of the water, the amount of dissolved solids in the water, the availability of light, the depth of the water, and the material at the bottom of the biome. Aquatic biomes are classified as marine or freshwater biomes based on the amount of dissolved salt in the water. **Marine biomes** include the intertidal zone, the pelagic zone, the benthic zone, the abyssal zone, coral reefs, and estuaries. Marine biomes have a salinity of at least 35 parts per thousand or 3.5%. **Freshwater biomes** include lakes, ponds, rivers, and streams. Freshwater biomes have a salinity that is less than 0.5 parts per thousand or 0.05%. Lakes and ponds, which are relatively stationary, consist of two zones: the littoral zone and the limnetic zone. The **littoral zone** is closest to the shore and is home to many plants (floating and rooted), invertebrates, crustaceans, amphibians, and fish. The **limnetic zone** is further from the shore and has no rooted plants. Rivers and streams typically originate in the mountains and make their way to the oceans. Because this water is running and colder, it contains different plants and animals than lakes and ponds. For example, salmon, trout, crayfish, plants, and algae are found in rivers and streams.

Marine Regions

Marine regions are located in three broad areas: the ocean, estuaries, and coral reefs. The ocean consists of two general regions—the pelagic zone and the benthic zone. The **pelagic zone** is in the open ocean. Organisms in the pelagic zone include phytoplankton such as algae and bacteria; zooplankton such as protozoa and crustaceans; and larger animals such as squid, sharks, and whales. The **benthic zone** consists of the ocean floor. Organisms in the benthic zone can include sponges, clams, oysters, starfish, sea anemones, sea urchins, worms, and fish. The deepest part of the benthic zone is called the **abyssal plain** and is usually very cold and dark. This is the deep ocean floor, which is home to numerous scavengers, many of which have light-generating capability. **Estuaries** are somewhat-enclosed coastal regions where water from rivers and streams is mixed with seawater. **Coral reefs** are located in warm, shallow water. Corals are small colonial animals that share a mutualistic relationship with algae.

Terrestrial Biomes

Terrestrial biomes are classified predominantly by their vegetation, which is primarily determined by precipitation and temperature. **Tropical rainforests** experience the highest annual precipitation and relatively high temperatures. The dominant vegetation in tropical forests is tall evergreen trees. **Temperate deciduous forests** experience moderate precipitation and temperatures. The dominant vegetation is deciduous trees. **Boreal forests** experience moderate precipitation and lower temperatures. The dominant vegetation is coniferous trees. The **tundra** experiences lower precipitation and cold temperatures. The dominant vegetation is shrubs. The **savanna** experiences lower precipitation and high temperatures. The dominant vegetation is grasses. **Deserts** experience the lowest precipitation and the hottest temperatures. The dominant vegetation is scattered thorny plants.

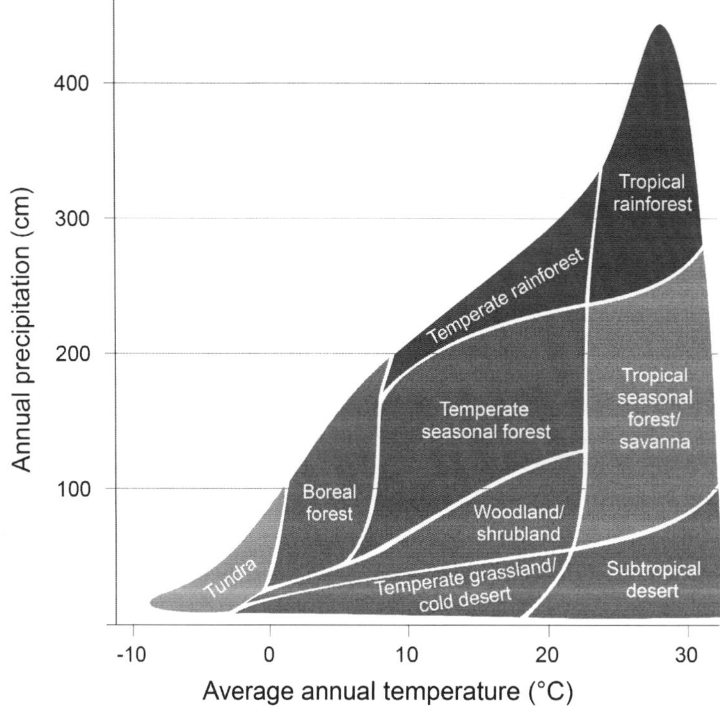

Natural Resources

The term **natural resources** refers to products and energy that can be harvested from the world and used.

- **Water** is one of the most abundant resources on the Earth and is necessary for life.
- **Natural gas** and **oil** exist underground and deep in the ocean and can be used as fuel for machines.
- **Trees** can be harvested for wood and paper and other byproducts that are used in daily life.
- **Metals** can be harvested from the ground and are used in many applications, such as building materials and in electronics.
- **Sand** can be used to make glass, soaps, and electronics.
- **Sunlight** and **wind** can be harvested with solar panels and wind turbines to generate electricity.
- **Animal products** are used for food or materials in clothing and some manufacturing processes.

Renewable and Non-renewable Resources

Materials and energy on the Earth are classified as either renewable or non-renewable. The term **renewable resources** refers to resources that are not going to run out due to overuse or can be easily reclaimed once used. This includes the sun, wind, and water. Some plants and animals grow so fast that it would be very challenging to run out and cause any form of extinction. **Non-renewable resources** include materials that take a very long time to produce, such as fossil fuels and coal. Once the Earth's population uses these materials up, it is very difficult to obtain or impossible to create more. Because renewable resources do not run out, whereas non-renewable resources do, environmentalists and scientists are always looking for new renewable resources to supply the planet with energy and for ways to reduce consumption of non-renewable resources. This reduction of consumption is known as **conservation**.

Environmental Impacts

Environmental Crises

As industrialization moves into developing countries, pollution and stripping of natural resources follows. The increased world-wide demand for goods means that countries are motivated more by monetary gain than environmental concerns. Forests are decimated, water and air polluted, but the global community has been unable to reach a worldwide agreement on environmental planning, resulting in increasingly common environmental problems.

Greenhouse Effect

The **greenhouse effect** refers to a naturally occurring and necessary process. **Greenhouse gases**, which are ozone, carbon dioxide, water vapor, and methane, trap infrared radiation that is reflected toward the atmosphere. Without the greenhouse effect, it is estimated that the temperature on Earth would be 30 degrees less on average. The problem occurs because human activity generates more greenhouse gases than necessary. Practices that increase the amount of greenhouse gases include the burning of natural gas and oil, farming practices that result in the release of methane and nitrous oxide, factory operations that produce gases, and deforestation practices that decrease the amount of oxygen available to offset greenhouse gases. Population growth also increases the volume of gases released. Excess greenhouse gases cause more infrared radiation to become trapped, which increases the temperature at the Earth's surface. Venus experiences a greenhouse effect similar to that observed on Earth as its dense atmosphere traps the solar radiation and creates a greenhouse effect. The greenhouse gases, including ozone, carbon dioxide, water vapor, and methane, trap infrared radiation that is reflected back toward the atmosphere. While both Venus and Earth experience the greenhouse effect, Venus's greenhouse effect is much more severe.

Ozone Depletion

Ultraviolet light breaks O_2 into two very reactive oxygen atoms with unpaired electrons, which are known as **free radicals**. A free radical of oxygen pairs with another oxygen molecule to form **ozone** (O_3). Ultraviolet light also breaks ozone (O_3) into O_2 and a free radical of oxygen. This process usually acts as an ultraviolet light filter for the planet. Other free radical catalysts are produced by natural phenomena such as volcanic eruptions and by human activities. When these enter the atmosphere, they disrupt the normal cycle by breaking down ozone so it cannot absorb more ultraviolet radiation. One such catalyst is the chlorine in chlorofluorocarbons (CFCs). CFCs were used as aerosols and refrigerants. When a CFC like CF_2Cl_2 is broken down in the atmosphere, chlorine free radicals are produced. These act as catalysts to break down ozone. Whether a chlorine free radical reacts with an ozone or oxygen molecule, it is able to react again.

Human Impacts on Ecosystems

Human impacts on **ecosystems** take many forms and have many causes. They include widespread disruptions and specific niche disturbances. Humans practice many forms of **environmental manipulation** that affect plants and animals in many biomes and ecosystems. Many human practices involve the consumption of natural resources for food and energy production, the changing of the environment to produce food and energy, and the intrusion on ecosystems to provide shelter. These general behaviors include a multitude of specific behaviors, including the use and overuse of pesticides, the encroachment upon habitat, over hunting and over fishing, the introduction of plant and animal species into non-native ecosystems, deforestation and clearing land for agriculture, logging, mining, and urbanization, and the introduction of hazardous wastes and chemical byproducts into the environment. These behaviors have led to a number of consequences, such as acid rain, ozone depletion, deforestation, urbanization, accelerated species loss, genetic abnormalities, endocrine disruption in populations, and harm to individual animals.

Global Warming

Global warming may cause the permanent loss of glaciers and permafrost. There might also be increases in air pollution and acid rain. Rising temperatures may lead to an increase in sea levels as polar ice melts, lower amounts of available fresh water as coastal areas flood, species extinction because of changes in habitat, increases in certain diseases, and a decreased standard of living for humans. Less fresh water and losses of habitat for humans and other species can also lead to decreased agricultural production and food supply shortages. Increased desertification leads to habitat loss for humans and other species. There may be more moisture in the atmosphere due to evaporation.

Acid Rain and Eutrophication

Acid rain is made up water droplets for which the pH has been lowered due atmospheric pollution. The common sources of this pollution are **sulfur** and **nitrogen** that have been released through the burning of fossil fuels. This can lead to a lowering of the pH of lakes and ponds, thereby destroying aquatic life, or damaging the leaves and bark of trees. It can also destroy buildings, monuments, and statues made of rock.

Eutrophication is the depletion of oxygen in a body of water. It may be caused by an increase in the amount of nutrients, particularly **phosphates**, which leads to an increase in plant and algae life that use up the oxygen. The result is a decrease in water quality and death of aquatic life. Sources of excess phosphates may be detergents, industrial run-off, or fertilizers that are washed into lakes or streams.

Waste Disposal Methods

- Landfills – **Methane** (CH_4) is a greenhouse gas emitted from landfills. Some is used to generate electricity and some gets into the atmosphere. CO_2 is also emitted, and landfill gas can contain nitrogen, oxygen, water vapor, sulfur, mercury, and radioactive contaminants such as tritium. **Landfill leachate** contains acids from car batteries, solvents, heavy metals, pesticides, motor oil, paint, household cleaning supplies, plastics, and many other potentially harmful substances. Some of these are dangerous when they get into the ecosystem.
- Incinerators – These contribute to air pollution in that they can release nitric and sulfuric oxides, which cause **acid rain**.
- Sewage – When dumped in raw form into oceans, sewage can introduce **fecal contaminants** and **pathogenic organisms**, which can harm ocean life and cause disease in humans.

Effects of Consumerism

Economic growth and quality of living are associated with a wasteful cycle of production. Goods are produced as cheaply as possible with little or no regard for the **ecological effects**. The ultimate goal is profitability. The production process is wasteful, and often introduces **hazardous byproducts** into the environment. Furthermore, byproducts may be dumped into a landfill instead of recycled. When consumer products get dumped in landfills, they can leach **contamination** into groundwater. Landfills can also leach gases. These are or have been dumping grounds for illegal substances, business and government waste, construction industry waste, and medical waste. These items also get dumped at illegal dump sites in urban and remote areas.

Energy Production

- **Coal-fired power plants**: These generate electricity fairly cheaply, but are the largest source of **greenhouse gases**.
- **Gasoline**: Gasoline is cheap, generates less CO_2 than coal, and requires less water than coal. But it nevertheless releases a substantial amount of CO_2 in the aggregate and is a limited resource. The burning of gas and other fossil fuels releases carbon dioxide (a greenhouse gas) into the atmosphere.
- **Nuclear power plants**: A small nuclear power plant can cheaply produce a large amount of electricity. But the waste is potentially harmful and a substantial amount of **water** is required to generate electricity. The cost of storing and transporting the **radioactive waste** is also very large.
- **Hydropower**: Hydropower is sustainable and environmentally benign once established. A disadvantage is that the building of a dam and the re-routing of a river can be very **environmentally disruptive**.
- **Wind power**: Wind power is sustainable, non-polluting, and requires little to no cooling water. But it will not produce power in the absence of **wind** and requires a large area over which the turbines can be laid out.
- **Solar power**: Solar power is sustainable, can be used for a single house or building, and generates peak energy during times of peak usage. But production is limited to when the sun is shining, the panels themselves are expensive to make, and making the panels generates harmful **toxins**.
- **Geothermal power:** Geothermal power is sustainable, relatively cheap, and non-polluting. Disadvantages are that it can only be utilized in areas with specific **volcanic activity**.

American Land Use for Transportation

In the United States, up to 70 percent of urban land is used for transportation—for parking lots, roads, and highways, as well as for light rail trains and subways and for airports. The national highway system includes about 160,000 miles. The areas devoted to automobile use have high concentrations of pollutants from gasoline and from wear and tear on tires, brake pads, and lubricating oil. Air pollutants from automobiles include hydrocarbons, carbon dioxide, carbon monoxide, nitrogen oxides, ozone, and volatile organic compounds (VOCs). Water is polluted by many of the same chemicals when it runs off the roads.

In some places, large areas are used for canals and channels that provide routes for transportation by water and/or reroute water to allow transportation by land. In Florida, canals cover thousands of miles; New Orleans is famous for its canals. In addition to navigation, canals are important for flood control and agricultural irrigation.

Overfishing

Efficient modern fishing methods (including GPS systems, spotter planes, and factory ships) and government subsidies allow more fish to be taken than in the past. The **larger fish species** (tuna, cod) have been harvested to the point where they are not as profitable. This has shifted the fishing to smaller individuals of the large species and then to smaller species of fish (mackerel). This is called **fishing down the food chain** (or web). Catching these smaller fish for human consumption makes them unavailable for the remaining larger fish, which fail to reestablish their populations. The result of this **overfishing** is that we are left with fewer and fewer food fish. Integrated coastal management programs and marine reserves can improve the numbers (and biodiversity) of fish in the ocean. The United Nations Convention on the Law of the Sea (UNCLOS) sets guidelines for sustainable use of ocean fishes. However, these guidelines are not followed by many fishing nations or by pirate fishers.

Effects of Burning Fossil Fuels on the Environmental

Burning fossil fuels (naturally-occurring hydrocarbon compounds that may be used by humans for fuel), especially coal, releases harmful elements into the atmosphere. The chemical reaction of coal combustion produces, for example, large amounts of carbon dioxide. When these gases reach the atmosphere, they inhibit the release of infrared photons into space—carbon dioxide molecules absorb the photons and may reflect them inward, back toward the Earth. This phenomenon is called the **greenhouse effect**. While the greenhouse effect is desirable, to a certain degree, to maintain a comfortable climate on the planet, increased levels of carbon dioxide can change the balance of energy in the atmosphere. This is termed **global warming**. Coal burning can also cause acid rain. Sulfur dioxide, a byproduct of burning coal, rises to the atmosphere and combines with water molecules to form sulfuric acid. This acid rain falls back to Earth, where it can cause harm to plants, animals, water bodies, and exposed structures. Burning gasoline can also contribute to the formation of acid rain.

Outdoor and Indoor Air Pollutants

The major outdoor air pollutants are carbon dioxide and carbon monoxide; sulfur dioxide and sulfuric acid; nitrogen oxides, nitric acid, and nitrates (or nitrate salts); particulates, or suspended particulate matter (SPM); ozone (at ground level); and VOCs (volatile organic compounds) such as hydrocarbons (including methane) and various solvents.

Indoor air pollutants include outdoor pollutants plus radioactive radon-222, cigarette smoke, cooking- and heating-fire smoke, formaldehyde, and very small particles.

Concentrations of most pollutants are measured in parts per million by volume (ppm or ppmv), milligrams per cubic meter of air (mg/m^3), or micrograms per cubic meter of air ($\mu g/m^3$). Radon is usually measured in picocuries per liter of air (pCi/L).

Water Pollution

Water pollution is a change in water that reduces the ability of water organisms to live in it or makes it unusable by humans. **Point source pollution**, as from the outflow pipe from a factory into a river, is traceable to a specific point, or polluter. **Nonpoint source pollution**, such as runoff from city streets, is spread out and cannot be traced to someone or somewhere specific. The top three sources of water pollution are agriculture, industry, and mining:

- Agriculture pollutes with water and sediments contaminated with such things as nitrates, phosphates, pesticides, oxygen-demanding wastes from plants and animals, and microbial pathogens such as viruses, bacteria, and protozoa.
- Industry pollutes with inorganic chemicals such as arsenic and mercury, organic chemicals such as petroleum products, and heat.
- Mining pollutes with sediments, sulfuric acid, and toxic chemicals, such as mercury and arsenic.

Eutrophication, death of aquatic organisms, buildup of toxins in fish, and early death for 3.2 million people per year are some effects of **water pollution**. Because many water sources are not suitable for human use, many countries purify their piped water as a government service. The first step is often holding the water in reservoirs to increase dissolved oxygen and decrease sediment. Commonly, the second step is disinfection with chlorine, ozone, or sunlight. Improving and maintaining water quality is a more sustainable way to provide potable water:

- In agriculture, organic farming would reduce nitrates, phosphates, and pesticides; oxygen-demanding plant and animal wastes would be composted for later application to the soil; this would keep many pathogens out of streams, and streamside areas could be kept planted to reduce erosion.
- In industry, arsenic, mercury, and other chemicals could be removed from industrial processes or reduced or at least removed from effluent (outgoing wastewater).

Watersheds

A **watershed** is a defined area where all the water from one place or multiple nearby places drains into a common location such as a river or ocean. A watershed is made up of two main types of water: surface water and ground water. **Surface water** is any water visible above ground, such as lakes and rivers, and **groundwater** is freshwater contained underneath the soil and fills the space between rocks and soil particles. Human activities can impact surface water through contamination, pollution, and the construction of dams. Human activities can also contaminate groundwater through the dumping of waste and the use of chemicals near the soil. Groundwater can also be depleted when people use wells to acquire drinking water. One of the most significant impacts on watersheds is **agricultural runoff**, which the result of fertilizers and pesticides from farms leaking into surface water and groundwater sources. Because all the water in a watershed drains into the same location, pollution present in any of the water sources can impact the entire watershed. This can potentially reduce the amount of freshwater available to humans and wildlife in an area.

Practice Test #1

1. Fossils are least likely to be found in which type of rock?

a. Sedimentary rock
b. Metamorphic rock
c. Igneous rock
d. Fossils are commonly found in all types of rock

2. Students are working in groups to complete an experiment their teacher assigned. The steps for the experiment are listed below.

Experiment Steps
1. Pour $\frac{1}{2}$ cup of hydrogen peroxide into an empty water bottle.
2. Add 1 teaspoon of dish soap to the water bottle.
3. Swirl the water bottle to mix the liquids.
4. In a small glass, mix 1 tablespoon of yeast and 3 tablespoons of warm water.
5. Pour the yeast mixture into the water bottle containing the hydrogen peroxide and dish soap.
6. Place your hand right above the water bottle and notice the heat coming from it.
7. Notice the foam rises in the water bottle and begins to overflow.

Which step above suggests that a chemical reaction occurred during the experiment?

a. Step 2: add 1 teaspoon of dish soap to the water bottle.
b. Step 3: swirl the water bottle to mix the liquids.
c. Step 5: pour the yeast mixture into the water bottle containing the hydrogen peroxide and dish soap.
d. Step 6: place your hand right above the water bottle and notice the heat coming from it.

3. How are igneous rocks formed?

a. Years of sediment are laid down on top of each other and forced together.
b. Acid rain caused by pollution creates holes in metamorphic rocks.
c. Dust and pebbles are pressed together underground from Earth's heat and pressure.
d. Magma from a volcanic eruption cools and hardens.

4. The category of elements that contains most of the semiconductors is called?

a. Metals
b. Metalloids
c. Nonmetals
d. Noble gases

5. Many water sports take place in the ocean. Some of these sports can negatively impact the aquatic populations in the areas where they take place. Those impacts not only hurt aquatic life, but they can also reduce human access to aquatic resources. Which of the following water sports is the most likely to have a negative impact on aquatic populations and resources?

a. Competitive surfing
b. Competitive sailing
c. Competitive fishing
d. Competitive swimming

6. The rainforest is home to thousands of different types of vegetation. There are four main levels of the rainforest as pictured below.

Which abiotic factor are the plants on the forest floor NOT competing with the other layers for?

a. Oxygen
b. Water
c. Sunlight
d. Fertile soil

7. Decide whether each of the actions below would increase or not increase the sustainability of an ecosystem in a city park. Write your answer for each action in the corresponding blank. The options are listed below.

Will increase sustainability	Will not increase sustainability

Action	Impact on Sustainability
Planting native shrubs about the perimeter of the park	
Spraying ant piles regularly to prevent bites	
Cutting shrubs regularly to prevent insect infestation	
Adding a pollinator garden	
Placing bird feeders in the trees	
Placing park benches around common areas of the playground	
Decreasing the number of trees to allow for more sunlight	

8. List the number of neutrons, protons, and electrons in ^{238}U.

a. 238, 92, 238
b. 92, 146, 146
c. 146, 92, 92
d. 92, 92, 146

9. The grasshopper population in a garden was completely wiped out when a farmer used an all-natural repellent to rid the garden of the grasshoppers since they were eating the tomato plants. The main source of food for the small lizards that also lived in the garden was grasshoppers. Which statement below describes the indirect effect the farmer's action most likely had on the lizards?

a. The lizard population in the garden increased because the competition for space with the grasshoppers had been eliminated.
b. The lizard population decreased because the tomato plants no longer provided adequate shelter.
c. The lizard population in the garden decreased because the lizards were forced to relocate to a different area where the grasshoppers weren't affected by the farmer's actions.
d. The lizard population in the garden stayed the same because the lizards were forced to find a new source of food in the environment.

10. In reference to the table below, if the state allowed hunting in only the highest populated years, what conclusions below would not have affected the continued decrease in population numbers from 1970 to 2010?

State Coyote Population, 1900-2010

Year	Population	Year	Population
1900	5,000	1960	50,000
1910	11,000	1970	70,000
1920	30,000	1980	50,000
1930	75,000	1990	40,000
1940	100,000	2000	20,000
1950	65,000	2010	8,000

a. Scarcity of food sources
b. Migration to another area
c. The prohibition of coyote hunting
d. Reduction of shelter

11. Which of the following describes two species that depend on a similar biotic and abiotic factor in their environment?

a. Giraffes eat the leaves of the acacia tree, while ants feed on the sap inside the same tree. Giraffes and ants both thrive in warm temperatures.
b. Grizzly bears and black bears in Yellowstone National Park feast on huckleberry plants and ants.
c. Sharks and dolphins both swim in the waters of the Pacific Ocean and prefer the water temperature to be fairly warm.
d. The yucca and the prickly pear both have root systems that thrive in sandy soil. Both plants need very little rain, making the desert an ideal environment them to live in.

12. Which two of the following are NOT results of a chemical reaction? Select all that apply.

a. Temperature change
b. Mass decrease
c. Melting
d. Bubbles
e. Precipitate forming

13. Which does NOT correctly explain a cause-and-effect relationship between tectonic plate boundaries and their effects on Earth?

a. The subduction boundary under the Pacific Ocean floor near Japan caused an underwater earthquake that led to a tsunami in 2011.
b. The Himalayas are a large mountain range in Asia that were formed long ago when tectonic plates of Eurasia and India collided at a convergent boundary.
c. The San Francisco Earthquake of 1906 was one of the deadliest earthquakes in US history and was located along a transform boundary.
d. The Rocky Mountains are a mountain range that runs through Colorado and were created by plate tectonics at a divergent boundary.

14. The lithification process results in the formation of which of the following types of rocks?

a. Sedimentary
b. Intrusive igneous
c. Extrusive igneous
d. Metamorphic

15. In the food chain pyramid below, which segment represents the placement of a coyote?

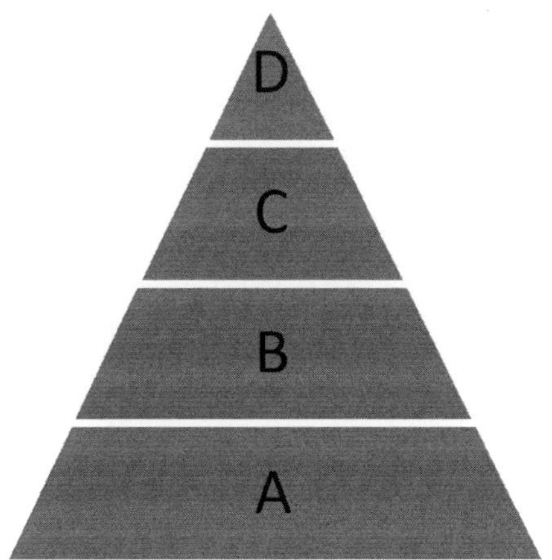

a. A (Producer)
b. B (Primary Consumer)
c. C (Secondary Consumer)
d. D (Decomposer)

16. Students created the energy web below to diagram the energy flow in an Arctic ecosystem.

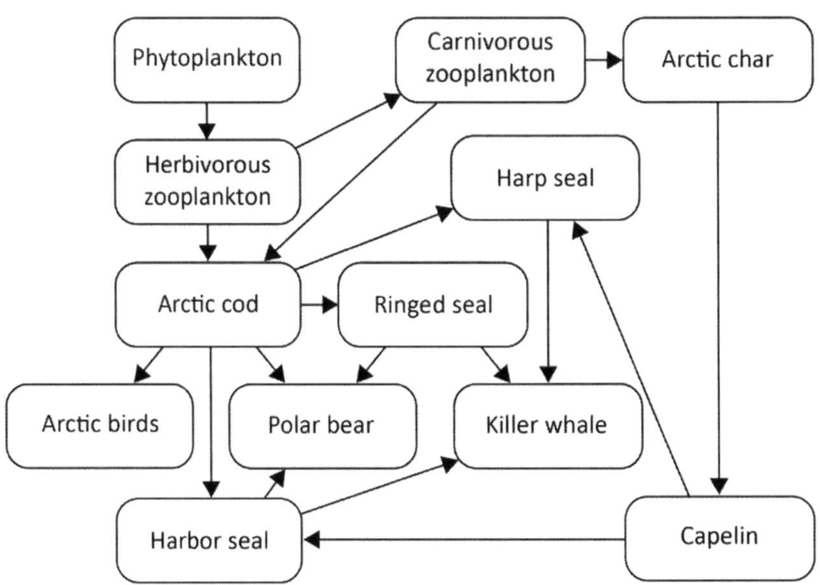

Based on the energy web, which statement is NOT true?

a. Harbor seals are the prey of polar bears and predators of arctic cod.
b. Killer whales prey on ringed seals and harp seals, but they do not have any predators.
c. Carnivorous zooplankton are the prey of arctic cod and herbivorous zooplankton but the predator of arctic char.
d. Polar bears are the predator of the ringed seal and the arctic cod, but they are not the prey of any other organism.

17. This butterfly has markings on its wings that look like huge eyes. How does this physical adaptation help the butterfly stay alive and reproduce?

a. The eyespots help the butterfly fly.
b. The eyespots help the butterfly find food.
c. The eyespots help the butterfly scare off predators.
d. The eyespots help the butterfly smell.

18. What is the name of the process by which plants generate their own food source using sunlight, carbon dioxide, and water?

a. Photoemission
b. Chemotherapy
c. Chemosynthesis
d. Photosynthesis

19. In the marine waters, there is a beautiful, orange clown fish that lives closely with a sea anemone. This sea anemone can sting its prey with poisonous venom before devouring it; however, the clown fish is not affected by the sea anemone at all. The clown fish is only safe when hiding within the sea anemone's poisonous tentacles and protects the hiding spot from a certain type of fish who tries to eat the sea anemone. This is an example of what type of relationship?

a. Commensalism
b. Mutualism
c. Parasitism
d. None of the above

20. When a volcano erupts, the lava may flow for miles. When the lava cools, it can create a new rocky environment. Which of the following species would be the last to move into an area where this type of primary succession had occurred?

a. Plants with no roots like mosses
b. An oak tree that has deep roots
c. A fungus like a lichen
d. A willow tree that has shallow roots

21. Which of the following is the most likely explanation for the reason finches on separate islands within an archipelago have differently shaped beaks?

a. Each bird evolved from a pre-existing ancestor on each island
b. The finches spread among the islands, but in small numbers, so genetic drift caused beak shape to change
c. Natural selection shaped the beaks in accordance with food availability on each island
d. The different finches were introduced by ancient humans

22. The images below show the Arctic Circle in 1979 and in 2003. Which of the following would not be a short- or long-term effect of this change?

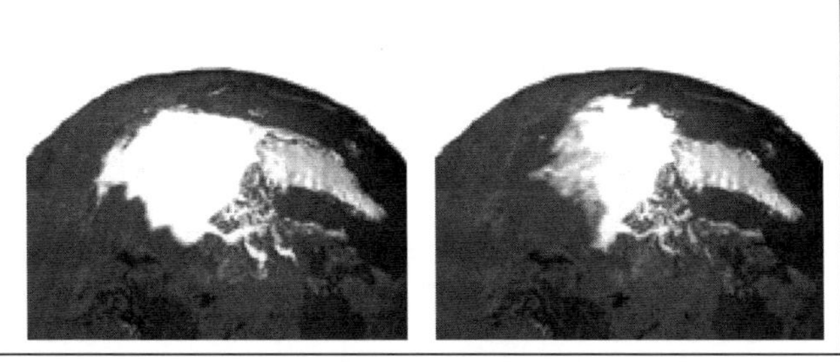

Arctic perennial sea ice has been decreasing at a rate of 9% per decade. The first image shows the minimum sea ice concentration for the year 1979, and the second image shows the minimum sea ice concentration in 2003.

a. Impact on the ecological food pyramids and webs
b. Increase in sea levels
c. Diminished wetlands and marshes around the world
d. Increased global temperatures for the land and oceans

23. Which of the following situations would result in the generation of new crust?

a. Two crustal plates converge
b. Two crustal plates move apart
c. Two crustal plates slide past one another
d. A crustal plate is pushed down into the mantle

24. Which of the following is a property of nonmetals?

a. They are good conductors of electricity
b. They do not form isotopes
c. They react with metals
d. They are dense, hard, and have high melting points

25. Metals, nonmetals, and metalloids have many similarities and differences. In the blank next to each characteristic in the table, write the category that characteristic matches. The options are listed below.

Metals only	Nonmetals only	Metals and metalloids	Nonmetals and metalloids

Characteristic	Category
Can appear shiny	
Insulator of heat	
Low melting point	
Can appear dull	
Excellent conductor of electricity	
Can conduct thermal energy	

26. Energy pyramids show different organisms in each trophic level of an ecosystem.

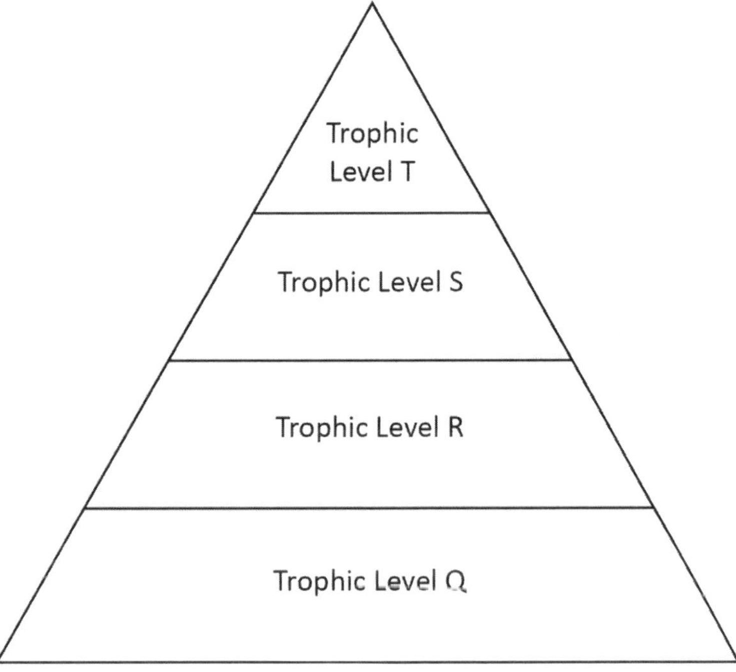

In the energy pyramid for the northern Pacific Ocean, which trophic level would algae and seaweed belong in? Which tropic level would killer whales belong in? Why would those organisms could belong in the trophic levels you chose? Write your response to these questions on the lines below.

27. Write the missing term from each sentence below in the blank beneath the sentence.

All elements in groups 3 to 12 in the periodic table can be classified as ____________.

Since these elements share that property, it can also be determined that these elements are good ____________ of heat and electricity.

28. Cells are the smallest unit of a living organism; therefore, atoms would be the smallest unit of _____.

a. Matter
b. Mass
c. Weight
d. Periodic Table

29. Balance the following reaction between sulfuric acid and aluminum hydroxide by filling in the correct stoichiometric values for each chemical.

$$\_\ H_2SO_4 + \_\ Al(OH)_3 \rightarrow \_\ Al_2(SO_4)_3 + \_\ H_2O$$

a. 3, 2, 1, 6
b. 2, 3, 1, 3
c. 3, 3, 2, 6
d. 1, 2, 1, 4

30. Which of the following statements is the best conclusion based on the data provided?

The fossilized remains of a bat have been found in volcanic rock dated to A.D. 79. Scientists studying the bat believe it to be an extinct species.

a. The volcanic eruption caused the extinction of this species of bat.
b. The only casualties from the eruption were bats.
c. The bat was probably from the same period as the volcanic eruption.
d. Bats never survive volcanic eruptions.

31. Using the Periodic Table, what is the total number of protons for iron? Write your answer in the blank below.

32. Which answer balances the following equation?

$CO_2 + H_2O + Energy = C_6H_{12}O_6 + O_2$

a. $12CO_2 + 6H_2O + Energy = C_6H_{12}O_6 + 6O_2$
b. $6CO_2 + 6H_2O + Energy = 2C_6H_{12}O_6 + 12O_2$
c. $12CO_2 + 6H_2O + Energy = 2C_6H_{12}O_6 + 6O_2$
d. $6CO_2 + 6H_2O + Energy = C_6H_{12}O_6 + 6O_2$

33. Periodic tables are useful for many reasons. One way they can be used is to help classify elements.

Element	Classification
____________	Metalloid
____________	Metal
____________	Noble Gas
____________	Nonmetal

Match each element to its classification using knowledge of the periodic table.

Rn – Radon	Cl – Chlorine
Co - Cobalt	B - Boron

34. A farmer noticed that his cornfield was being destroyed by grasshoppers. He researched many ways to eliminate grasshoppers from his fields and noticed several good options. Which option would most negatively affect the quality of the water in his area?

a. Removing weeds and other overgrowth from the area so only soil and corn stalks remain
b. Using a commercial pesticide
c. Spraying the plants with a water and garlic solution
d. Lightly dusting the corn plants with flour

35. Which of the following scenarios is NOT an example of a chemical reaction?

a. The eggs, oil, and brownie powder were mixed and placed in the hot oven. The batter began rising as more heat was added.
b. The banana sitting on the counter began developing black spots all over its surface.
c. The puddle on the ground evaporated, and the concrete was no longer wet.
d. A tablespoon of vinegar was poured into a container of baking soda, and then bubbles and foam formed and spilled out onto the table.

36. Which of the following is a true statement about the Earth's oceans?

a. Oceans comprise about 50% of the Earth's surface.
b. The deepest point in the ocean is about 6,000 meters below sea level.
c. The ocean is divided geographically into four areas: the Atlantic, Pacific, Mediterranean, and Indian.
d. The ocean's salinity is usually between 34 and 35 parts per thousand, or 200 parts per million.

37. What are pure substances that consist of more than one type of atom?

a. Elements
b. Compounds
c. Molecules
d. Mixtures

38. Oxygen is an element that is found in many different substances. Oxygen is found in the balanced equation that the student wrote below.

$$2Fe_2O_3 + 3C \rightarrow 4Fe + 3CO_2$$

Which balanced equation shows a reaction that has the same number of oxygen atoms as the balanced equation the student wrote above?

a. $6Fe + 3O_2 \rightarrow 2Fe_3O_3$
b. $4Ca + 4CO_3 \rightarrow 2Ca_2 + 2C_2O_6$
c. $8Fe + 4O_2 \rightarrow 4Fe_2O_2$
d. $4Ca_3 + 2CO_2 \rightarrow 6Ca_2 + C_2O_4$

39. Scientists studied a forest ecosystem where most of the plants were dying and only a few were still living. Below are some notes the scientists took.

Dying Plants	**Living Plants**
Number of plants: 50-60 Root depth: shallow (1-2 ft) Other observations: • Dried-up leaves • Dying plants clumped together	Number of plants: 5-6 Root depth: deep (6-8 ft) Other observations: • Roots are spread out • Plants not near each other

Based on the notes, why might most of the plants be dying while only a few are living?

a. The lack of oxygen is causing plants to die. The living plants have deeper roots, which give them more access to oxygen below the soil, but the dying plants have less access to oxygen because of the shallow roots.
b. The lack of Sun is causing the plants to die. The shallow root system of the dying plants doesn't allow as much access to the Sun as the deep root system of the living plants.
c. The increase in insects is causing the plants to die. Since the dying plants are all clumped together, there are more insects living in those plants eating the stems and leaves.
d. The lack of water is causing the plants to die. The large number of plants with shallow roots is causing too much competition for water. There are only a few plants with a deeper root system, and those plants are far apart, so there is little competition among them.

40. Which three substances below contain eight or more atoms? Select all that apply.

a. $2CaC_2$
b. $2C_2H_2$
c. $3CaCl_2$
d. H_3PO_4
e. H_2CO_3

41. All of the following are examples of chemical changes in the digestive system except

a. Converting starches in carbohydrates to simple sugars
b. Protein digestion in the stomach
c. Chewing food into smaller pieces
d. Digestion of fat in the small intestine

42. Place the following elements in order of decreasing electronegativity:

N, As, Bi, P, Sb

a. As > Bi > N > P > Sb
b. N > P > As > Sb > Bi
c. Bi > Sb > As > P > N
d. P > N > As > Sb > Bi

43. Which of the following statements is NOT congruent with the theory of plate tectonics?

a. The continents were once connected in the large supercontinent Pangea.
b. The tectonic plates are part of the Earth's lithosphere.
c. Seafloor spreading is evidence of tectonic plate movement.
d. Subduction occurs at divergent boundaries.

44. Which of the following would not be used as evidence for evolution?

a. Fossil record
b. DNA sequences
c. Anatomical structures
d. Reproductive habits

45. Which of the following sources of fresh water is generally NOT available for human consumption?

a. Rivers
b. Estuaries
c. Aquifers
d. Glaciers

46. Which of the following is a source of nonrenewable energy?

a. Solar power
b. Wind power
c. Wood
d. Coal

47. Which of the following layers of the earth make up the lithosphere?

a. The crust only
b. The crust and the rigid upper portion of the upper mantle
c. The crust and the upper mantle
d. The crust, upper mantle, and lower mantle

48. All of the following are true regarding wind energy, EXCEPT:

a. Wind turbines use space inefficiently, but they have low operational costs.
b. Wind is not a reliable source of energy in all geographic locations.
c. Wind turbines are expensive to manufacture and install.
d. Wind turbines are a threat to wildlife.

49. Which type of rock typically forms on the surface of the Earth in cumulative layers?

a. Igneous
b. Obsidian
c. Metamorphic
d. Sedimentary

50. ______________________ are nonliving, infectious particles that act as parasites in living organisms.

a. Bacteria
b. Viruses
c. Fungi
d. Protozoa

51. Which of the following is not a way to prevent the spread of diseases?

a. Vaccinations
b. Personal Protective Equipment
c. Avoiding cold weather
d. Maintain good hygiene

52. Which of the following is a renewable source of energy?

a. Wind
b. Natural gas
c. Crude Oil
d. Coal

Answer Key and Explanations for Test #1

1. C: Fossils are least likely to be found in igneous rock. Igneous rock is formed by extreme heat as magma escapes through the Earth's crust and cools. The remains of plants and animals in fossil form are not usually preserved under these conditions. Sedimentary rock (A) is where most fossils are found. Sedimentary rock is formed more slowly and is very abundant. Since soft mud and silts compress into layers, organisms can also be deposited. Metamorphic rock (B) is rock that has undergone a change by heat and pressure. This usually destroys any fossils, but occasionally fossil remains are simply distorted and can be found in metamorphic rock.

2. D: Step 6 of the experiment states the ingredients in the bottle are producing heat, which is a temperature change. A temperature change is a sign that a chemical reaction has happened. Adding dish soap, mixing the liquids, and combining mixtures do not, on their own, suggest a chemical reaction has occurred.

3. D: Igneous rocks are formed when magma in the Earth erupts through cracks in the crust. There, the lava cools, creating a hard structure with many air pockets or holes.

4. B: An element that has semi-conductive properties would be a metalloid. Metals are good conductors of electricity and heat. In contrast, nonmetals and the noble gases are not good conductors of electricity and heat. A semi-conductor is one that will conduct electricity under some conditions, but not others.

5. C: Competitive fishing is the most likely of these sports to cause disruptions and harm to aquatic populations and ecosystems. Fishing requires removing fish from the ocean, and though many fish caught for sport are released back into the water, many are not returned to the site where they were caught. These fish may not be able to return to their original location and may not survive if they were harmed when they were caught or during transport in the boat. Additionally, most competitive fishing is done using motorboats, which can release harmful chemicals into ocean waters and harm aquatic populations. Options A and B are incorrect because, although surfing and sailing might have some negative impacts on aquatic populations and resources, they are much less harmful than competitive fishing. Option D is incorrect because swimming is also not very disruptive to marine life.

6. A: The plants on the forest floor are covered by three other layers of vegetation and are competing for water, sunlight, and fertile soil space. Since these plants are on the bottom, they must adapt the most to receive the abiotic factors they need to survive. Oxygen flows freely throughout all levels.

7.

Action	Impact on Sustainability
Planting native shrubs about the perimeter of the park	Will increase sustainability
Spraying ant piles regularly to prevent bites	Will not increase sustainability
Cutting shrubs regularly to prevent insect infestation	Will not increase sustainability
Adding a pollinator garden	Will increase sustainability
Placing bird feeders in the trees	Will increase sustainability
Placing park benches around common areas of the playground	Will not increase sustainability
Decreasing the number of trees to allow for more sunlight	Will not increase sustainability

The sustainability of the park ecosystem would be increased through the creation of more biodiversity. This could be done by adding living elements such as shrubs, a pollinator garden to attract bees and butterflies, and bird feeders to attract birds. The sustainability would decrease by killing ants, shrubs, and trees, since these actions would limit biodiversity. Placing park benches has no effect on sustainability.

8. C: The mass number is the number of protons and the number of neutrons added together. The number of protons is also known as the atomic number and can be found on the periodic table. Therefore, the number of neutrons is the mass number (238) less the number of protons (92), so there are 146 neutrons. The number of electrons always equals the number of protons in a neutral atom, so C is the correct answer.

9. C: The main food source for the lizards in the garden was the grasshoppers. With the grasshoppers eliminated, the lizards had to move to a new area where the grasshoppers weren't affected by the farmer's actions. Therefore, the population of lizards in the garden decreased. The extra space did not help the lizards because the main food source was gone. The tomato plants were not affected in this scenario. In this situation, most lizards would not adapt their eating habits but would instead find a new location.

10. C: Although no data is shown that reflects the years in which hunting licenses were sold, the prohibition of hunting would allow a population to increase its numbers. The coyote's populations would suffer without adequate food sources or shelter, and migration would reduce it as well.

11. A: Giraffes and ants both eat from the acacia tree, which is a biotic factor since it is living. They both also need warm temperatures, which is an abiotic, or nonliving, factor. The bears both interact with the same biotic factors. The shark and dolphins both interact with the same abiotic factors, as do the desert plants.

12. B, C: When a chemical reaction occurs, the mass remains unchanged. Melting is a sign of a physical change. Temperature change (A), development of odor, bubbles (D), the formation of a precipitate (E), and a color change are all signs a chemical reaction could have happened.

13. D: Divergent boundaries do not form mountains but instead cause the tectonic plates to move away from each other, often creating ocean ridges. Tsunamis like the one in Japan in 2011 are caused by underwater earthquakes at subduction boundaries. Mountains like the Himalayas are often formed at convergent boundaries, which appear where tectonic plates push together. The San Francisco Earthquake in 1906 happened along a transform boundary, and this type of boundary appears where tectonic plates slide past each other.

14. A: The lithification process results in the formation of sedimentary rocks. During lithification, existing rock is compacted and liquid is squeezed from its pores. Eventually, the rock is cemented together, resulting in sedimentary rock.

15. C: The diagram represents an ecological pyramid. The letter A represents the producers, such as plants. The letter B represents the primary consumers usually herbivores. The letter C stands for the secondary consumers, the carnivores that feed on the herbivores. A coyote is a carnivore and would, therefore, be in this group and represented by the letter C. The pyramid's fourth level, represented by a D, includes the decomposers, such as bacteria and fungi, which decompose dead organic material.

16. C: Option C is the correct answer because according to the arrows in the diagram, carnivorous zooplankton are the prey of arctic char and arctic cod and predators of herbivorous zooplankton. Option A is not the correct answer because the arrows indicate that harbor seals are the prey of polar bears and the predators of arctic cod. Option B is not the correct answer because the arrows indicate that killer whales prey on ringed seals and harp seals, but they do not have a predator. Option D is not the correct answer because the arrows indicate that polar bears are predators of ringed seals and artic cod, but they do not have any predators.

17. C: The eyespots help the butterfly scare off predators. Butterflies with the two large eyespots will suddenly show them to predators to scare them off. The eyespots do not help them fly, find food, or smell. These spots help the butterfly stay alive and reproduce, and this trait then becomes more prevalent. The butterflies without the eyespots will begin to decrease in number. Thus, this is an example of natural selection.

18. D: Photosynthesis is the process by which plants generate their own food (glucose), using sunlight, water, and carbon dioxide. Oxygen is also generated as a byproduct.

19. B: The relationship between the clown fish and the sea anemone is an example of mutualism - because both organisms are benefitting from the relationship. The Clown fish gains the protection from the anemone while offering protection to the anemone from being eaten by a certain type of fish.

20. B: An oak tree would be the last of the species listed to move into the area. It would take a long time for the rocky terrain to break down enough to suit the deep root system of an oak tree. The other species listed would be suited to the environment sooner after it is created. The fungus and the plants with no root systems would appear before the oak tree because they can adapt to grow on rocks. It would still take much time for the environment to change to support a willow tree, but because its roots grow to cover a wide area rather than growing deep into the ground, this environment could still support a willow tree before it could support an oak tree.

21. C: Finches with beaks well-suited for the types of food available on an island had an evolutionary advantage. As a result, these finches survived and reproduced, a phenomenon known as natural selection. The finches share a common ancestor, regardless of the island on which they now live. Genetic drift refers to genetic changes that occur due to random chance; this would not account for different beaks on different islands. Introduction by humans would not account for different beaks, since phenotypes change over time.

22. C: The melting of the Arctic Circle would mean that sea levels would increase and wetlands and marshes would then become flooded with seawater. This would lead to the death of many plant and animal species within those ecosystems. Global temperatures would not decrease but would increase on both the land and oceans.

23. B: When two crustal plates move apart, magma welling up could result in the formation of new crust. This has been shown to be occurring on the ocean floor where places of the crust are weaker. The crust spreads apart at these trenches, pushing outward and erupting at the ridges. When two crustal plates converge, sublimation occurs as one plate runs under another pushing it up. Two crustal plates slide past one another, is an example of a transform fault, which does not create new crust. A crustal plate is pushed down into the mantle, does not form new crust but perhaps recycles the old one.

24. C: Nonmetal ions are negatively charged, while metal ions are positively charged. Because of these opposite charges, they readily bond and react. The metal iron, for instance, reacts readily with the nonmetal oxygen to form rust. As a general rule, nonmetals are considered nonconductors Nonmetals, including oxygen, can form isotopes. Nonmetals typically have low densities, are not hard, and have low melting points.

25.

Characteristic	Category
Can appear shiny	Metals and metalloids
Insulator of heat	Nonmetals only
Low melting point	Nonmetals only
Can appear dull	Nonmetals and metalloids
Excellent conductor of electricity	Metals only
Can conduct thermal energy	Metals and metalloids

Only metals are excellent conductors of electricity, but metals and metalloids can conduct thermal energy and can be shiny in appearance. Only nonmetals insulate heat and have a low melting point, but nonmetals and metalloids can appear dull. Metalloids can appear either shiny or dull.

26. Energy pyramids show how energy is distributed in an ecosystem. Producers often have the most energy, so they are usually represented at the bottom of the pyramid. Trophic level Q represents organisms that are producers, so algae and seaweed would belong in that level. Each tier or level has less energy than the one beneath it, so the organisms represented at the top of the pyramid are consumers. In this pyramid, the top level represents tertiary consumers. Trophic level T represents tertiary consumers, which are predators of secondary consumers, so a killer whale would belong in that level.

27. metals, conductors: All the elements located in groups 3 to 12 are metals. Metals have properties that make them good conductors of heat and electricity.

28. A: Atoms are the smallest and most basic unit of matter. When combined, they form elements just as cells of the same type form tissues.

29. A: By comparing the products to the reactants, there must be at least two Al atoms in the starting material, and at least three sulfate groups. Therefore, a coefficient of 2 must be placed in front of $Al(OH)_3$ and a coefficient of 3 must be placed in front of H_2SO_4. To make the number of hydrogen and oxygen atoms equal on both sides of the equation, a coefficient of 6 must be placed in front of H_2O.

30. C: If the bat was found in the lava from a volcanic eruption dated in 79 A.D., it is a reasonable conclusion that the bat came from that period.

31. 26: On the Periodic Table, iron (Fe) has an atomic number of 26 and an atomic mass of 55.847. The atomic number indicates the number of protons that the element has within its nucleus. The atomic mass is the average mass of the isotopes within that element. The answer is 26 protons because the atomic number is 26.

32. D: The equation $6CO_2 + 6H_2O + \text{Energy} = C_6H_{12}O_6 + 6O_2$ (photosynthesis) can be balanced by counting the number of each element on the reactant side and comparing those totals to the product side. There should be equal numbers of each element on both sides, and they can be adjusted by changing the coefficient to add another molecule to the formula to balance the other side. The formula above represents photosynthesis and has six more CO_2 molecules on its reactant side than usual; thus, additional glucose and oxygen molecules will be produced.

33.

Element	Classification
B - Boron	Metalloid
Co - Cobalt	Metal
Rn - Radon	Noble Gas
Cl – Chlorine	Nonmetal

Boron is located in group 13 of the periodic table. It falls in the "stair-step" portion of the table, so it is a metalloid. Cobalt is located in group 9 of the periodic table. Most of the elements in groups 1 through 12 are metals. Radon is located in group 18. This group houses all the noble gases. Chlorine is located in group 17 above the "stair-step" portion of the table, so it is a nonmetal.

34. B: Commercial pesticides have chemicals that can get into groundwater and pollute area streams and lakes. Removing weeds and overgrowth would not affect the water in the area. The water and garlic solution and the flour would enter the water supply, but since neither contain harsh chemicals, they would not be harmful.

35. C: Evaporation is a physical change and does not result in a chemical reaction. The ingredients of the brownie were mixed, and when heat was added, a new substance was formed, which is evidence of a chemical reaction (A). Any rotting fruit is an example of a chemical reaction (B). Over time, air reacts with the yellow banana skin to create a chemical reaction that results in the black, rotting spots. When vinegar and baking soda are combined, new substances are formed, which is evidence that a chemical reaction occurred. The bubbles are also an indicator of a chemical reaction (D).

36. D: It is true that the ocean's salinity is usually between 34 and 35 parts per thousand, or 200 parts per million. Oceans comprise about 70.8% of the Earth's surface, and the ocean's deepest point is over 10,000 meters below sea level. The Mediterranean is considered a sea, not an ocean.

37. B: Elements and compounds are both pure substances. Elements consist of only one type of atom. Compounds consist of more than one type of atom. Molecules may make up either elements or compounds. Mixtures are two or more substances that are physically combined but not chemically united.

38. A: The balanced equation in the example contains six oxygen atoms on both sides of the arrow. Option A is a balanced equation that has six oxygen atoms on both sides. Option B contains 12 oxygen atoms. Option C contains eight oxygen atoms. Option D contains 4 oxygen atoms.

39. D: Since there are so many plants with a shallow root system, the plants are all competing for water, which is creating a water deficit. There are only a few plants with deep roots, and there is much less competition for water among them. The shallow root system does not result in less oxygen or less sunlight for plants, so that is not the cause of the plants dying. There is no evidence in the notes of an increase in the number of insects or signs of insect damage on the dying plants.

40. B, C, D: The first option contains only six atoms, so it is incorrect. The second option contains eight atoms, so it is correct. The third option contains nine atoms and is correct. The fourth option contains eight atoms and is correct. The fifth option contains only six atoms and is incorrect.

41. C: Chewing food into smaller pieces is a physical change, not a chemical change.

42. B: The trend within any column of the periodic table is that electronegativity decreases going down the column.

43. D: Subduction occurs at convergent boundaries. Subduction is the process that occurs when two tectonic plates collide and one plate moves under the other plate.

44. D: Reproductive habits would not be considered evidence for evolution. Usually, how a species reproduces does not support nor add to the body of evidence for the theory of evolution. Reproductive habits might exemplify how any given organism can adapt to changes in its environment as a way to survive. This does not necessarily show evolution. Fossil record is evidence for evolution as it shows evolutionary change of organisms over time. DNA sequences show that organisms that are related evolutionarily also have related gene sequences. Anatomical structures such as having an internal bony structure provide evidence of descent from a common ancestor.

45. B: Fresh water suitable for drinking can be found as surface water and in groundwater, which is obtained through wells. Rivers (surface water) and aquifers (groundwater) are both sources of fresh water that are available to humans. Glaciers and ice caps are indirect sources of fresh water–when they melt, the runoff forms streams and rivers. Water from all of these sources is suitable for drinking with little to no treatment. Estuaries, however, are not sources of fresh water; they are bodies of brackish (moderately salty) water formed where freshwater from a river mixes with salt water from an ocean. This water is not suitable for drinking without treatment such as desalinization.

46. D: Sources of renewable energy include geothermal power, solar energy, and wind power. Sources of nonrenewable energy include nuclear power and fossil fuels like coal, natural gas, and crude oil.

47. B: The lithosphere is the solid outer section of the earth. This includes the crust and the upper portion of the upper mantle. The asthenosphere, which lies in the upper mantle, is below the lithosphere.

48. A: Pros of wind energy include space efficiency, no pollution, and low operational costs. Cons of wind energy include wind fluctuation, threats to wildlife, and the expense to manufacture and install.

49. D: Sedimentary rock is formed on the surface of the Earth and deposited in layers as the result of natural processes like erosion. Igneous (A) rocks are formed from volcanic eruptions. Obsidian (B) is just one type of igneous rock. Metamorphic (C) rocks form deep in the Earth's crust through heavy pressure and/or heat, which metamorphose or change sedimentary and igneous rocks far below the surface.

50. B: Viruses are nonliving, infectious particles that act as parasites in living organisms. Bacteria are infectious; however, they are living and cellular. Fungi can cause diseases as well, but they are also living organisms. Protozoa are single-celled eukaryotes, but they can be parasitic.

51. C: Avoiding cold weather does not help prevent the spread of diseases. Viruses and bacteria spread through contact, droplets, and contaminated surfaces. Some ways to prevent the spread of diseases are through vaccinations, personal protective equipment, and proper hygiene.

52. A: Wind is a renewable source of energy, because there will always be wind. Natural gas, crude oil, and coal will eventually run out and are nonrenewable. Therefore, the correct choice is A.

Practice Test #2

1. Which of the following elements are ordered from least reactive to most reactive according to the Periodic Table?

a. Ar, Cu, Na
b. Na, Ar, Cu
c. Na, Cu, Ar
d. Ar, Na, Cu

2. Rocks are classified as *igneous, metamorphic,* or *sedimentary* based on:

a. How they were formed
b. Their texture
c. The minerals they contain
d. Their age

3. Which of the following is an example of a chemical change?

a. Salt dissolving in water
b. Water evaporating
c. Silver tarnishing
d. Dry ice sublimating

4. Which of the following answers shows $CH_4 + O_2 = CO_2 + H_2O$ as balanced?

a. $CH_4 + 2O_2 = 2CO_2 + 2H_2O$
b. $2CH_4 + 4O_2 = 2CO_2 + H_2O$
c. $2CH_4 + O_2 = 2CO_2 + H_2O$
d. $CH_4 + 2O_2 = CO_2 + 2H_2O$

5. Scientists believe that the southern part of Florida was underwater during the Jurassic period. What evidence would best support this?

a. The southern part of Florida is covered by sea.
b. Scientists discover erosion in the area.
c. *Tyrannosaurus rex* fossils are not discovered in the area.
d. Scientists discover fossils of aquatic species in the area.

6. Evidence of a chemical reaction can be determined by all of the following except?

a. Modifying the arrangement of atoms
b. Endothermic and exothermic reactions
c. Equal masses of reactants and products
d. No change in energy

7. English ivy is a vine that is native to Ireland and grows and multiplies quickly. English ivy vines wrap themselves around the trunks of trees and continue to grow over the branches and leaves. They can easily cover an entire tree from the ground up, damaging the bark, and they will compete with the tree for sun and water.

How might the growth of English ivy affect the ecosystem of a wooded area over time?

a. The ivy will provide additional shelter for animals living in the wooded area.
b. The trees overtaken by the ivy will eventually die, and the tree population will decrease.
c. The trees will benefit from the extra moisture that the ivy traps.
d. The ivy will strengthen the trees and help them grow more quickly.

8. A student was given a solid object and made observations about it. Based on the observations provided, classify the solid as a metal or metalloid, and determine if this object conducts electricity.

Classification	Conductivity	Observation 1	Observation 2	Observation 3
____________	____________	Not malleable & broke easily when hammered	Shiny, reflective luster	High melting point

Match the correct response to the location in the table. Not all options will be used.

Metalloid	Metal
Conductor	Does not conduct electricity
Semiconductor	

9. Which of the following would not be considered a force driving the rock cycle?

a. Plate tectonics
b. The water cycle
c. Global warming
d. Volcanic eruptions

Refer to the following for questions 10-11:

Mount Everest is the tallest mountain, above sea level, in the world.

10. Which image below shows how tectonic plates interact to form mountains like Mount Everest?

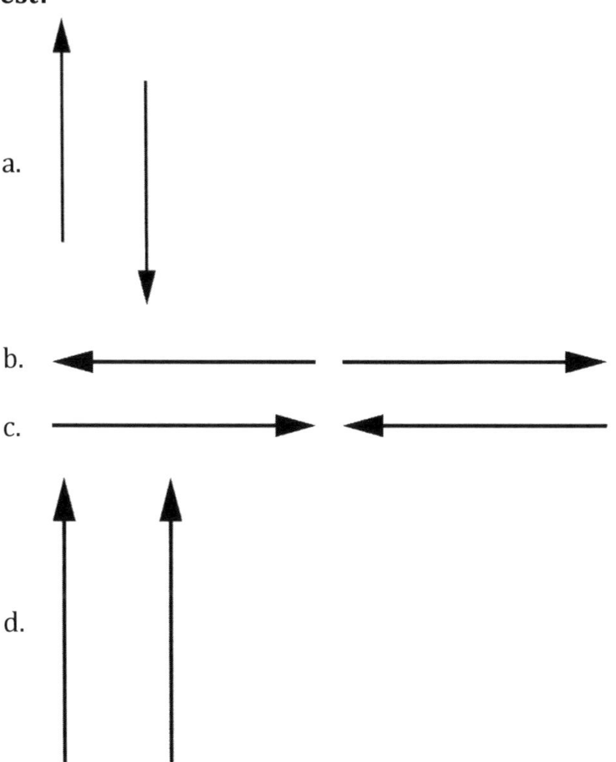

11. Which term correctly identifies the type of boundary identified in the previous question that can result in the formation of a mountain?

a. Divergent boundary
b. Transform boundary
c. Fault boundary
d. Convergent boundary

12. Below is a food web of marine organisms.

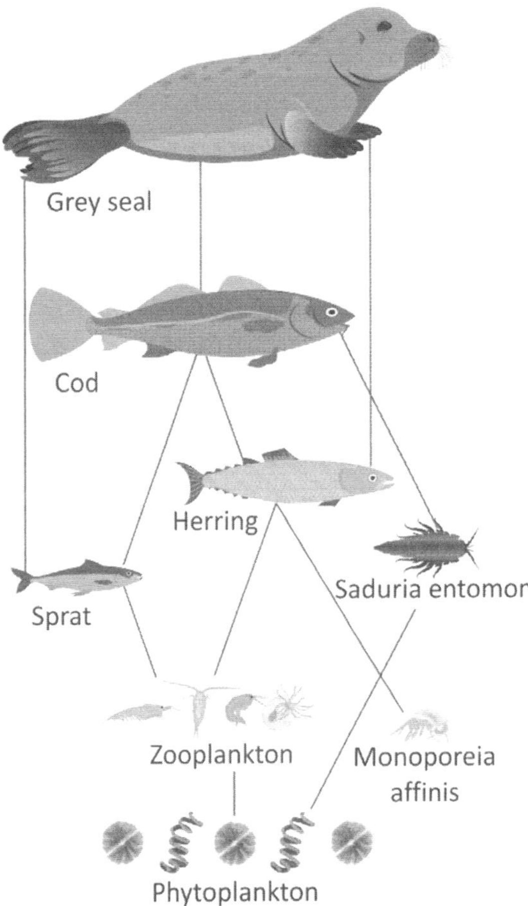

According to the food web, which correctly describes the flow of energy within these marine animals?

a. Phytoplankton → sprat → zooplankton → herring → gray seal
b. Zooplankton → sprat → cod → herring → gray seal
c. Cod → sprat → zooplankton → phytoplankton
d. Phytoplankton → *Saduria entomon* → cod → gray seal

13. Which of the following is an example of an experiment that shows a chemical change?

a. A clear liquid is poured into a beaker. A different clear liquid is poured into the same beaker. A wooden stir stick is used to mix the liquids together. Small, solid flecks begin to fall to the bottom of the beaker.
b. A liquid and a solid are combined in a beaker. The solid dissolves in the liquid. Heat is added. Eventually, only a solid remains at the bottom of the beaker.
c. A liquid and a solid are combined in a beaker. The beaker is shaken, and the solid dissolves. Then the beaker is placed in the freezer. Two hours later it is removed, and a solid has formed.
d. Two clear liquids are combined in a beaker. The beaker is then placed on a heater. Gas begins to rise from the beaker.

14. A student writes the clues about an element below.

Element Clues:
1. Has seven valence electrons 2. Has 10 neutrons 3. Has nine electrons 4. Has nine protons

What element is the student describing?

a. Neon, (Ne)
b. Argon, (Ar)
c. Silicon, (Si)
d. Fluorine (F)

15. Examine each circled set of elements and classify each set as metals, nonmetals, metalloids, or rare earth elements. For each set, fill in the bubble that corresponds to the correct similarity from the options below.

a. Metals
b. Metalloids
c. Nonmetals
d. Rare Earth Metals

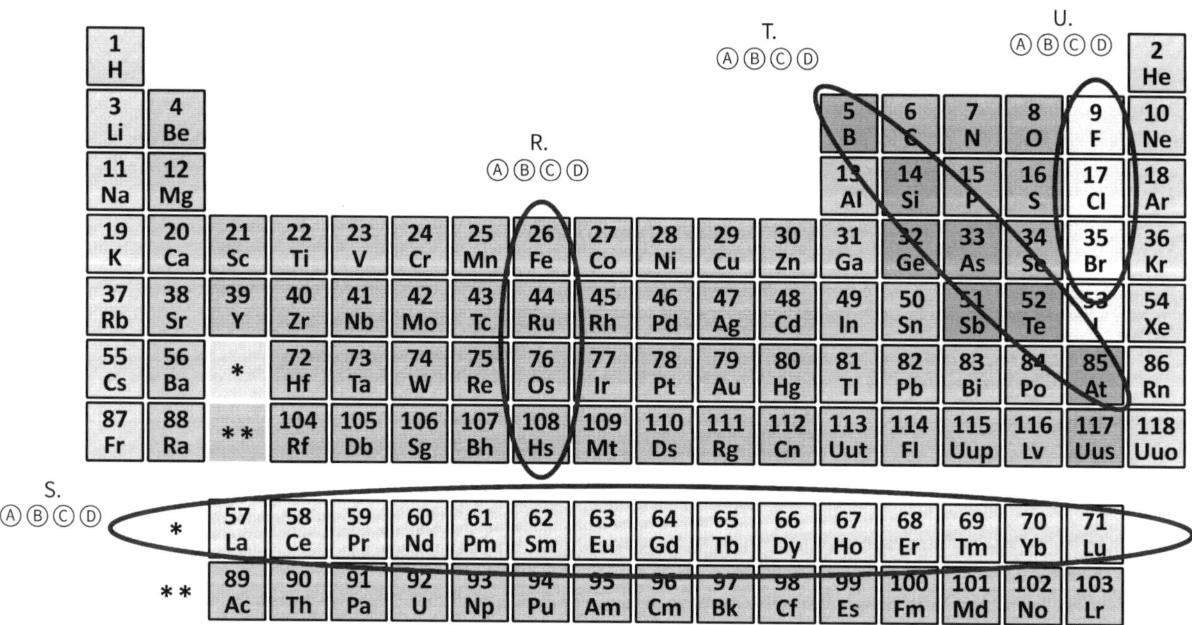

16. Which of the following is not an example of a renewable resource?

a. Sunlight
b. Crude oil
c. Wind
d. Tide

17. Coral reefs are an important ecosystem within the world's oceans. They act as a filtering system, reduce the amount of carbon dioxide in the water, provide shelter for many organisms, and offer economic benefits to many people around the world. However, coral reefs are in danger of being irreversibly destroyed. Which of the following is not a cause of the destruction of coral reefs?

a. Reattachment of salvaged coral colonies on the reef
b. Global warming
c. Collection of coral by people to sell
d. Water pollution

18. A desert biome is depicted below showing the biotic factors organisms rely on for food.

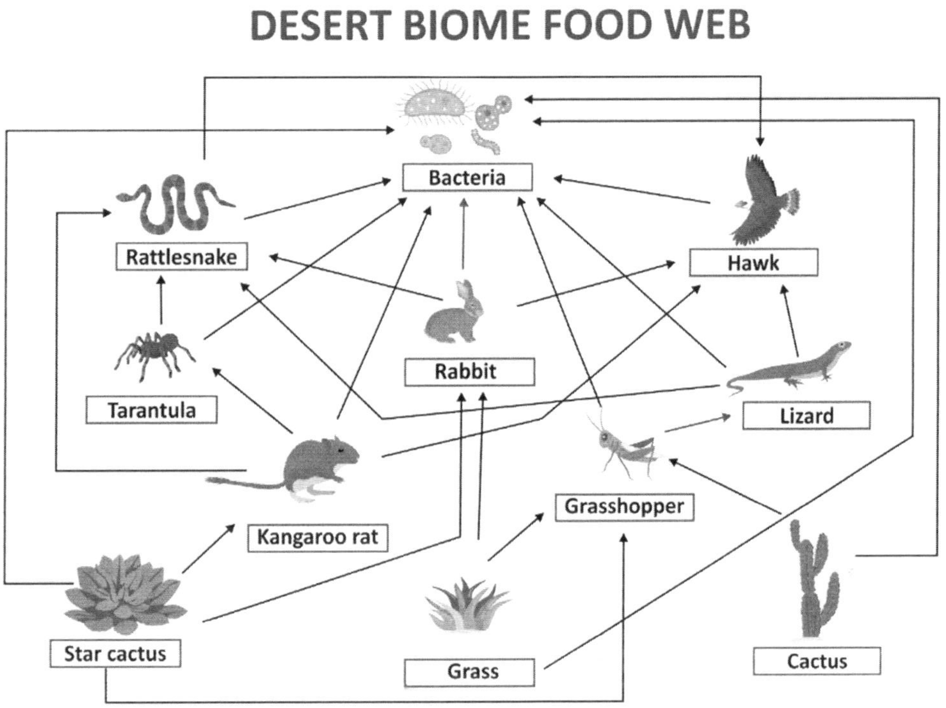

DESERT BIOME FOOD WEB

What would be the result if something happened to drastically decrease the grasshopper population in the desert biome?

a. The plants would not be eaten by another organism on the food web.
b. The kangaroo rat population would decrease since there would be fewer plants to eat.
c. The lizard population would drastically decrease as well.
d. The lizard population would increase since the population of one of its predators would have decreased.

19. Which of these refers to the oceans and water areas of Earth?

a. Atmosphere
b. Hydrosphere
c. Exosphere
d. Lithosphere

20. A seagull is a medium-sized bird that can be found flying above coastlines, bays, and lakes, and it is an omnivore. A hammerhead shark is a special category of fish and can grow to be over 500 pounds. It lives in the ocean and is a carnivore. Which is NOT a biotic factor that seagulls and hammerhead sharks compete for?

a. Cod fish
b. Seaweed
c. Mussels
d. Shrimp

21. On average, how many neutrons does one atom of bromine (Br) have?

a. 35
b. 44.90
c. 45
d. 79.90

22. Which of the following below is not considered evidence of plate tectonics?

a. The shape of continents fits together like a puzzle
b. Fossil comparisons exist along where the continents would fit together
c. The Mid-Atlantic Ridge shows where new crust is formed
d. There is a large amount of inland seismic activity

23. Before a factory was built in town, the population of moths was 90 percent white and 10 percent gray. After the factory was built, the population of moths changed to 20 percent white and 80 percent gray. The factory releases smoke into the air, which leads to air pollution in town. Which answer choice best describes the change in the moths' colors?

a. The factory covered the white moths' wings in soot.
b. The gray color is better suited to the new smoke-polluted environment.
c. The moths decided to change color so that they would be less visible.
d. The gray moths are predators of the white moths.

24. Bluefin tuna are a species of fish that need ocean water below 68 degrees Fahrenheit to survive. Global warming is causing the oceans' temperatures to change. The graph below illustrates this change.

How might the population of bluefin tuna adapt to this environmental change?

a. The bluefin tuna will have to adapt to survive closer to the surface of the ocean water where the temperatures are warmer.
b. The bluefin tuna will have to move to bodies of freshwater where the water temperatures are colder than 68 degrees.
c. The bluefin tuna will have to decrease their daily movement to stay cooler in the warming water.
d. The bluefin tuna will have to adapt to survive at a deeper ocean depth where the water temperatures are cooler.

25. The atomic number of an element is determined by:

a. The number of neutrons in the nucleus of an atom
b. The number of protons in the nucleus of an atom
c. The number of protons plus the number of neutrons in an atom
d. The number of protons plus the number of electrons in an atom

26. A tapeworm lives within another organism and feeds off the nutrients that are ingested by that organism. At times, this can cause the organism to experience malnutrition or death. This is an example of what type of relationship?

a. Predator/prey
b. Symbiosis
c. Parasite/host
d. Producer/consumer

27. In a pond, eutrophication, the pollution of water by plant nutrients, can occur, causing chemical, biological, and ecological changes to the pond. As plant material begins to decompose and carbon dioxide begins to increase, what would happen to the fish in the pond?

a. They would flourish
b. They would relocate to another area
c. They would die off
d. They would not be affected

28. In Lake Erie, a species of fish called the Blue Pike was overfished one year. The following year, there was a pollution incident that killed off another large portion of the population. These events, combined with the previous year's overfishing of adult fish, led to the extinction of the Blue Pike species—none of the other species were affected. What happened to other fish species in the lake over time after the Blue Pike became extinct?

a. They became extinct
b. They were not affected by the other species' fate
c. Their numbers increased due to lack of competition
d. Their numbers decreased due to lack of competition

29. Our planet's oceans are experiencing climate changes, pollution, and overfishing. Which of the following answers is not a result of human activity?

a. Diminishment of coral reefs
b. Destruction of food webs
c. Increased population of all species
d. Degradation or total loss of wetlands

30. The San Andreas Fault runs for over 800 miles along the California coastline and is a transform boundary. Which statement below is true about California due to its location along the San Andreas Fault?

a. California is home to over 25 active volcanoes.
b. There are many earthquakes in California.
c. California is home to many hurricanes.
d. The land in California is home to many valleys.

31. All of the following are examples of physical changes in the digestive system except:

a. Squeezing the food through the esophagus
b. Drinking to help aid in swallowing food
c. Chewing food into smaller pieces
d. Digestion of fat in the small intestine

32. How many electrons are in an uncharged atom of $^{45}_{20}Ca$?

a. 20
b. 45
c. 65
d. 25

33. Two species of finches are able to utilize the same food supply, but their beaks are different. They are able to coexist on an island because of:

a. Niche overlap
b. Character displacement
c. Resource partitioning
d. Realized niches

34. How does the law of conservation of mass relate to the substances in a chemical reaction? Write your response to this question on the lines below.

____

____

____

____

____

35. Most of the energy in a food chain is concentrated in the level of the

a. primary producers
b. primary consumers
c. secondary consumers
d. tertiary consumers

36. Which of the following causes of ocean destruction is not a result of human activity?

a. Diminishment of coral reefs
b. Destruction of food webs
c. Increased population of all species
d. Degradation or total loss of wetlands

37. In the plate movement known as ____, an oceanic plate slides underneath a continental plate.

a. faulting
b. spreading
c. subduction
d. converging

38. Which of the following does not represent a physical change?

a. Salt dissolved in water
b. A spoiling apple
c. Sugar dissolved in water
d. Pulverized rock

39. In the suburban neighborhood of Northwoods, there have been large populations of deer, and residents have complained about them eating flowers and garden plants. What would be a logical explanation, based on observations, for the large increase in the deer population over the last two seasons?

a. Increased quantity of food sources
b. Decreased population of a natural predator
c. Deer migration from surrounding areas
d. Increase in hunting licenses sold

40. Wind farms are one source of alternative energy, energy that can be used in place of fossil fuels. The amount of energy a wind farm produces is determined by

a. Sunlight
b. Season
c. Wind
d. Rainfall

41. In a food chain, where does energy go after the secondary consumer dies?

a. Back to the Sun
b. To the producers
c. Into the air, becoming wind
d. To decomposers

42. Which of the following is a nonrenewable resource?

a. water
b. oxygen
c. sunlight
d. oil

43. Which of the following is false regarding solar energy?

a. Solar energy is environmentally friendly
b. Solar energy has the greatest conversion efficiency
c. Solar energy is low maintenance
d. Solar energy is silent

44. Which of the following is NOT a correct representation of the average salinity of seawater?

a. 35 parts per thousand
b. 3.5 parts per hundred
c. 3.5%
d. 35%

45. Illness that is wide spread throughout multiple countries or the whole world is referred to as a ________________.

a. Epidemic
b. Contagion
c. Endemic
d. Pandemic

46. Which of the following is a negative impact of reservoirs or dams?

a. Higher likelihood of flooding
b. Decreased dissolved oxygen
c. Increased rate of soil erosion
d. Less protection of water from pollution

47. How does the loss of biodiversity directly impact the environment and society?

a. Increase of access to raw materials
b. Increase of access to clean water
c. Decrease of food supply
d. Decrease of vulnerability to natural disasters

48. Which of the following statements generally describes the trend of electronegativity on the periodic table of elements?

a. Electronegativity increases going from left to right and from top to bottom.
b. Electronegativity increases going from right to left and from bottom to top.
c. Electronegativity increases going from left to right and from bottom to top.
d. Electronegativity increases going from right to left and from top to bottom.

49. Which of the following objects could be made of metal? Select all that apply.

☐	Object 1	solid	soluble in water	insulator of thermal energy	nonmagnetic
☐	Object 2	solid	insoluble in water	conductor of thermal energy	magnetic
☐	Object 3	solid	soluble in water	conductor of thermal energy	magnetic
☐	Object 4	solid	insoluble in water	insulator of thermal energy	nonmagnetic

50. Gazelles are an important biotic factor in the life of an African lion because they are one of the lion's main sources of food. The graph below shows the gazelle population compared to the lion population.

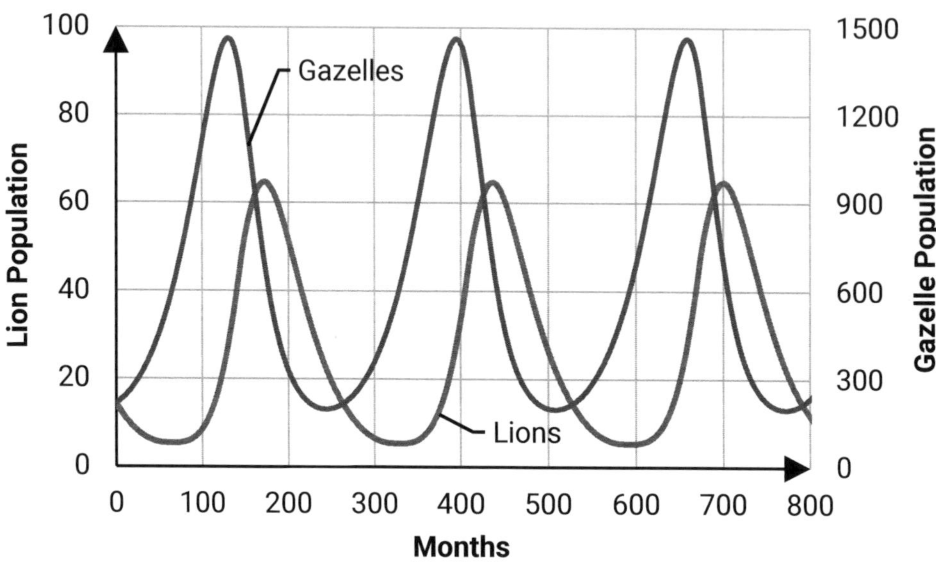

What is true about the gazelle population when the lion population is low? What is true about the gazelle population when the lion population is high? What is the reason for this? Write your response to these questions on the lines below.

____

____

____

____

____

51. Of the following, which is the most basic unit of matter?

a. A helium atom
b. A sodium ion
c. A proton
d. An oxygen molecule

52. Students are making observations about different elements. In the table, write the classification that best fits each element, based on its location on the periodic table. The options are listed below.

Metal	Nonmetal	Noble Gas

Element	Classification
Nickel (Ni)	
Xenon (Xe)	
Radon (Rn)	
Neon (Ne)	
Silicon (Si)	

Answer Key and Explanations for Test #2

1. A: The Periodic Table's two most reactive groups are Group 1 and Group 17; therefore, Na, found in Group 1, would be the most reactive of the three elements. The element Cu is found in Group 11, which marks it as a transition metal, and is only somewhat reactive. Group 18, which includes Ar, contains the Noble Gases, which are not at all reactive.

2. A: Igneous rocks form from the solidification of molten rock; metamorphic rocks form from changes in heat, pressure, or chemical activity; and sedimentary rocks are formed mainly by the compaction of rock fragments and other materials. All three types of rock may vary in texture, age, and mineral content.

3. C: A chemical change involves a chemical reaction where new products are formed. When silver tarnishes, a thin layer of corrosion is formed, indicating a chemical change. A physical change does not produce new substances. Phase changes such as evaporation and sublimation are examples of physical changes. Salt dissolving in water is also a physical change because the ions just separate, and no new substances are formed.

4. D: For the formula $CH_4 + O_2 = CO_2 + H_2O$ to be balanced there must be an equal number of molecules on both the reactant and product sides. In this case, for the formula to be balanced, a coefficient of a 2 needs to be placed in front of the O_2 and the H_2O molecules.

5. D: The best evidence to support the theory that Florida was once underwater would be fossils of aquatic species. If the state was underwater during the Jurassic period, animal and/or plant remnants from that era would be proof of this. Fossils of aquatic species would show the changes that have occurred to the environment over time. Answer choice A is incorrect because the southern part of Florida being covered in the present would not be evidence of whether Florida was underwater in the past. Answer choice B is incorrect because the erosion could have been caused by any number of things, including rain, wind, ancient glaciers, or flowing water in the present day. Answer choice C is incorrect because finding no evidence of one type of land dinosaur in the area does not mean that area was underwater. Instead of trying to explain why evidence is not present, scientists usually make conclusions based on evidence at hand. Therefore, finding evidence of aquatic animals is more convincing than not finding evidence of a land-dwelling animal.

6. D: A chemical reaction will always have an endothermic (absorb energy) or exothermic (release energy) reaction, and a chemical formula must always be balanced. Therefore, the masses of the reactants and products will always be equal, resulting in the modification of the atoms arrangement and a change in energy.

7. B: The English ivy will overtake the trees and use the water and sunlight that the trees need to survive. Eventually, the trees will die under the cover of the English ivy, and the population of trees will decrease. The ivy will lead to animals losing shelter because the trees will die. The ivy will use the water that the trees need to live, not provide more water. The ivy chokes the trees and does not provide support.

8.

Classification	Conductivity	Observation 1	Observation 2	Observation 3
Metalloid	Semiconductor	Not malleable & broke easily when hammered	Shiny, reflective luster	High melting point

Since the object was not malleable, it cannot be a metal. Shiny luster and a high melting point are characteristics that both a metal and a metalloid can have. Metalloids are semiconductors of electricity, and metals are better conductors of electricity.

9. C: In order to change the structure and form of rocks, intense or sustained changes must occur. Plate tectonics cause intense heat and pressure to modify rock structures. The water cycle can affect cooling and erosion that will also affect this cycle. Volcanic eruptions lead to melting and reforming in a more effective way than would global warming, which is a much more gradual process.

10. C: The arrows in option C show the plates coming together, which would force one or both parts of land up to form a mountain. Option A shows the plates sliding past one another. Option B shows the plates moving away from each other. Option D shows the plates moving in the same direction.

11. D: The boundary identified in the previous question that results in mountain formation is a convergent boundary. Referring to the options in the previous question, options A and D are both transform boundaries, and option B is a divergent boundary.

12. D: Option D is correct because it correctly lists the organisms from producers to consumers. Option A is incorrect because the zooplankton does not consume the sprat. Option B is incorrect because the herring does not consume the cod. Option C is incorrect it lists the organisms from consumers to producers.

13. A: In option A, two liquids are combined, and a new solid substance is formed. This is an example of a chemical reaction. In option B, a solid is dissolved in a liquid. The liquid is then evaporated by the heat, and the solid remains. This experiment shows only physical changes. Options C and D also both involve a change of state of matter, which is not an indication that a chemical reaction occurred.

14. D: It is understood that fluorine has seven valence electrons since it is located in group 17 of the periodic table. It can be determined that fluorine has 10 neutrons by subtracting fluorine's atomic number (9) from its mass number (19). Since fluorine has an atomic number of 9, it can be determined that it contains nine protons, and, as a neutral atom, it must also have nine electrons.

15.

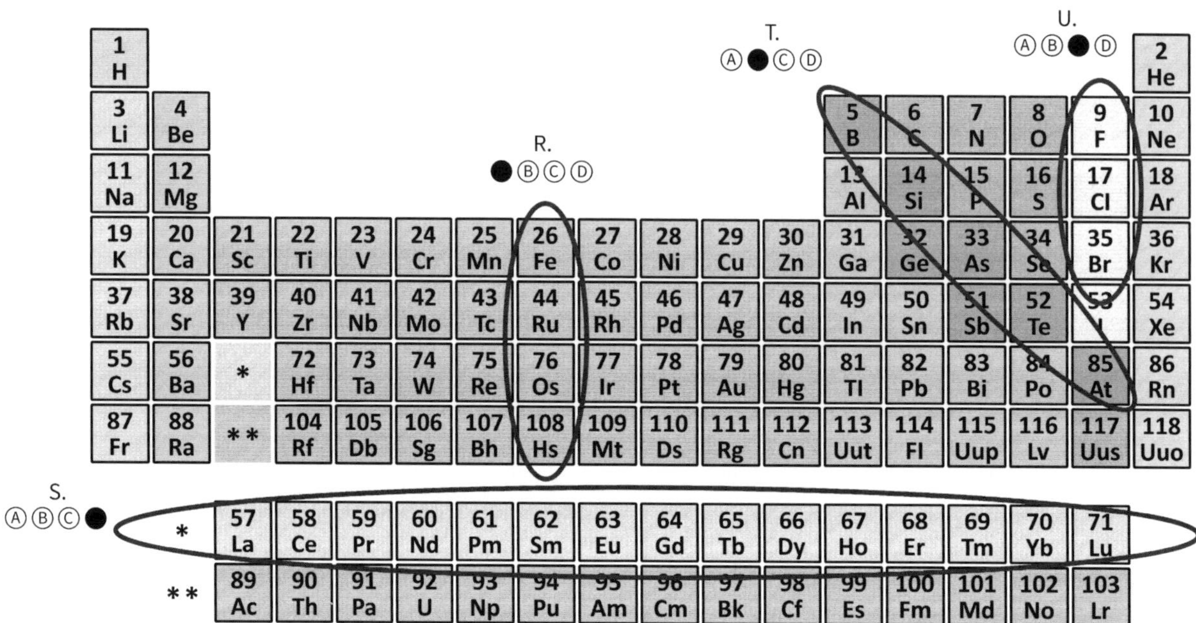

Elements in set R are all metals. Elements in set S are all rare earth metals. Elements in set T are all metalloids. Elements in set U are all nonmetals.

16. B: Renewable resources are those resources whose supplies can replenish naturally as quickly as or more quickly than they are consumed. Examples of renewable resources are sunlight, tides, and wind, which occur naturally and are plentiful. Fossil fuels take many years to form and are currently being consumed faster than they are being produced.

17. A: Coral reefs are destroyed by increased temperatures resulting from global warming and water pollution, which suffocates the coral as algae grows over it. Illegal collection and sale of coral to restaurants, pet stores, and others have depleted healthy colonies. Many conservation efforts include enacting international laws protecting the reefs, creating natural parks, and reattaching salvaged coral colonies on the reef with the hopes of reconstructing the reef have been started in recent years.

18. C: The lizard population would drastically decrease as well because the grasshopper is the main biotic factor the lizard depends on for food. The plants are still consumed by the rabbit and kangaroo rat. The kangaroo rats would have more plants to eat because they would no longer be competing with the grasshoppers. The grasshopper is not a predator of the lizard.

19. B: The Earth's environment consists of the atmosphere (the air we breathe), the hydrosphere (water), and the lithosphere (the land).

20. B: Seagulls are omnivores, meaning they eat plants and animals, but hammerhead sharks are carnivores, meaning they only eat meat. This means seagulls and hammerhead sharks would not compete for seaweed, since it is a plant. They both eat cod fish, mussels, and shrimp, so they would compete for these biotic factors.

21. B: To determine the average number of neutrons in one atom of an element, subtract the atomic number from the average atomic mass. For bromine (Br), subtract its atomic number (35) from its average atomic mass (79.9) to acquire the average number of neutrons, 44.9.

22. D: Evidence of plate tectonics is based on the shapes of the continents, which seem to fit together like a puzzle, as well as the fossils found along these edges. The Mid-Atlantic Ridge is the birthplace of new crust that is then destroyed in the subduction zones in the Pacific Ring of Fire, where most seismic activity takes place.

23. B: After the factory was built, it began polluting the town with smoke, making the environment grayer. In the new environment, it is likely that the gray moths would have an evolutionary advantage because they cannot be seen as well by predators as the white moths. Even without knowing the specifics, the change in numbers of white and gray moths can be attributed to environmental adaptation because the change happened after an environmental occurrence. Answer choice A is incorrect. While it is possible for a moth's wings to become covered in soot from the smoke, this is not something that would carry through generations. There is a difference between a physical change and a genetic change. A genetic change is passed through generations, whereas a physical change is not. Answer choice C is incorrect because genetic changes cannot occur based on want. Just as a person cannot decide to change eye color, a moth cannot decide to change the color of its wings. Answer choice D is incorrect because moths are not predators in the first place. Furthermore, these moths are different color variations of the same species, so they would not prey on each other.

24. D: The ocean waters are warming. The bluefin tuna population will have to adapt to survive at a deeper ocean depth where the waters are cooler. The waters at the surface of the ocean will be warmer, so that would not help the bluefin tuna. Bluefin tuna are saltwater fish and will not survive in freshwater. Decreasing movement will not affect temperature change enough.

25. B: The atomic number is equal to the number of protons in the nucleus, which is equal to the number of electrons. The number of protons plus the number of neutrons is equal to the mass number of the atom.

26. C: A parasite is an organism that feeds off the nutritional assets of another living thing called the host, which can lead to the host becoming malnourished or dying. Symbiosis occurs when there is a benefit to both organisms. A predator eats its prey. A producer produces food in the form of plant material that is eaten by a consumer.

27. C: In a pond, plants produce oxygen as a byproduct of photosynthesis. During eutrophication, plants die and decompose, causing increased levels of carbon dioxide. Fish cannot relocate from the pond, and they cannot live without oxygen, so they would die.

28. C: In an ecosystem, when one species is affected by overfishing or pollution, other species will either thrive due to a lack of competition or become extinct for the same reasons. The question states that the other species were not impacted by the overfishing or pollution. Thus, their populations would not have decreased for those reasons. Once extinct, the other species were no longer the potential prey of the Blue Pike or competing against them for similar food sources and so had the opportunity to increase their population numbers.

29. C: Human activities have not influenced the increased population of all species but have all played a role in the other environmental issues. As wetlands are degraded or lost, many ecosystems and species will also be lost, interrupting their respective food webs. Food webs within the actual oceans will also be reduced due to pollution and climate changes that impact water temperatures and levels. The diminishment of coral reefs means the ocean's water filtration system will be reduced or totally destroyed, affecting the ecosystems themselves as well as the organisms that use the area for breeding and feeding.

30. B: The San Andreas Fault is a transform boundary, and transform boundaries often cause earthquakes. Therefore, there are many earthquakes in California. Convergent boundaries are responsible for volcano formation and can also cause earthquakes, but California only has seven active volcanoes, and these were not formed due to California's location along the San Andreas Fault. Hurricanes are caused by weather and not plate boundaries. Valleys are caused by divergent boundaries.

31. D: Digestion of food in the small intestine occurs by bile secreted by the liver. This is a chemical change.

32. A: Since the atomic number is 20, which represents the number of protons in the atom, there must be an equal number of electrons in a neutral atom. Protons have a positive charge and electrons are negative. Equal numbers of protons and electrons will result in a neutral atom, or zero charge.

33. D: Species may theoretically be able to inhabit a particular area, called its fundamental niche. But the presence of competing species may mean that it only occupies part of its niche, called a realized niche.

34. The law of conservation of mass states that matter cannot be created or destroyed. This means that in a chemical reaction, new matter is not created, which would result in a greater mass, nor destroyed, which would result in a lower mass. In a chemical reaction, a new substance is formed, but no matter is created or destroyed in this process. The atoms have just been grouped in a new way. Therefore, the mass of the new substance would be the same as the mass of the previous substance.

35. A: A food chain shows how energy is transferred from one organism to another. A producer uses the energy from the sun to make its own food. Most of the energy in a food chain is in the level of the producer.

36. C: Human activities have not influenced the increased population of all species but have all played a role in the other environmental issues. As wetlands are degraded or lost, many ecosystems and species will also be lost, interrupting their respective food webs. Food webs within the actual oceans will also be reduced due to pollution and climate changes that impact water temperatures and levels. The diminishment of coral reefs means the ocean's water filtration system will be reduced or totally destroyed, affecting the ecosystems themselves as well as the organisms that use the area for breeding and feeding.

37. C: In the plate movement known as subduction, an oceanic plate slides underneath a continental plate. Oceanic plates are denser, so they tend to go beneath when they are pressed against lighter continental plates. The edge of the oceanic plate will be melted by the earth's mantle and may reemerge as a volcano. The Cascade Range of the northwest United States was formed by subduction. In faulting, the edges of two plates grind against each other laterally. The San Andreas Fault in California is perhaps the most famous example of this process. In spreading, plates pull apart from each other, typically creating a rift valley and the potential for earthquakes. In converging, two plates of similar density press against each other, creating mountain ranges where they meet.

38. A: Orange red stars have temperatures less than 3,700 K. Yellow orange stars range between 3,700 and 5,200 K. Yellow white stars range between 5,200 and 6,000 K. Blue white stars range between 10,000 and 30,000 K.

39. B: A decrease in a natural predator, such as a wolves, coyotes, bobcat, or wild dogs, would allow the population to become out of control. In a population of deer that has increased, there would be a natural decrease in a food source for the nutritional needs for the animals. Although deer have been known to share a human's developed habitat, it is often forced by reduced territory and food sources. An increase in hunting licenses would be used by local officials to try to control the population, helping to decrease the number of adults of breeding age.

40. C: Wind farms harvest energy from wind to use in combination with or in place of fossil fuels. The biggest limiting factors for wind farms are the inconsistency and unpredictability of wind and the difficulties involved in storing the energy that has been harvested. Wind farms can only produce as much energy as they receive from wind.

41. D: After a secondary consumer dies, such as a wolf, its body is partially consumed by decomposers, such as bacteria and fungi. Bacteria and fungi live in soil and digest body tissues of dead organisms, converting them into basic nutrients that plants need to grow. Therefore, after secondary consumers die, their energy is consumed by decomposers, who make nutrients available in the soil for producers to use. *Do not confuse nutrients in the soil with energy that producers get from the Sun to make their own food.*

42. D: Oil is a nonrenewable resource because it can not be replenished as quickly as it is used up. Water (A) is used frequently, but is replenished through the water cycle. Oxygen (B) is also used often, but is replenished through processes like plant respiration. Sunlight (C) is constantly provided by the sun and currently functions as an unlimited resource.

43. B: Pros of solar energy include the facts that it is renewable, abundant, environmentally friendly, low maintenance, and silent. Cons of solar energy include that it is expensive and intermittent and requires a lot of space. Solar panels require rare minerals like indium and tellurium and at this point are only about 20% efficient in harvesting energy—putting them behind several other alternative methods. Other solar harvesting methods besides the photoelectric effect include concentrated solar and water heating.

44. D: The average salinity of seawater is 3.5%. This can also be written as 35 parts per thousand or 3.5 parts per hundred.

45. D: A pandemic is wide spread illness throughout multiple countries or the whole world. An epidemic is confined to a specific region. An endemic is used to describe an illness that is constantly present in a specific area. Contagion refers to the process in which an illness spreads.

46. B: Water moves more slowly downstream of a dam. This results in less aeration and diffusion and lowers the dissolved oxygen content in the water.

47. C: The loss of biodiversity destabilizes ecosystems and impacts society by decreasing the food supply, decreasing the access to raw materials and clean water, and increasing the vulnerability to natural disasters.

48. C: The most electronegative atoms are found near the top right of the periodic table. Fluorine has a high electronegativity, while Cesium, located near the bottom left of the table, has a low electronegativity.

49.

☐	Object 1	solid	soluble in water	insulator of thermal energy	nonmagnetic
☒	Object 2	solid	insoluble in water	conductor of thermal energy	magnetic
☐	Object 3	solid	soluble in water	conductor of thermal energy	magnetic
☐	Object 4	solid	insoluble in water	insulator of thermal energy	nonmagnetic

A metal object could have the following characteristics: solid, insoluble in water, and conductor of thermal energy. Metal can be magnetic or nonmagnetic, so the last column cannot be used to eliminate any answer choices. Only object 2 has properties that match the properties of metals. Object 1 could not be made of metal because metal is insoluble, not soluble, in water, and metal is a conductor of thermal energy, not an insulator. Object 3 could not be made of metal because metal is insoluble, not soluble, in water. Object 4 could not be made of metal because metal is a conductor of thermal energy, not an insulator.

50. When the lion population is low, the gazelle population is high. The lion is a predator of the gazelle. When there are fewer lions, fewer gazelles will become prey, so more gazelles will live. When the lion population is at its highest, the gazelle population decreases because there are more lions to prey on the gazelles.

51. C: The most basic units of matter are protons, electrons, and neutrons. Protons are found in the nucleus, and have a positive charge. They are one of the three components of a helium atom a. When atoms have positive or negative charges, they are known as ions b. Molecules of oxygen, water, etc. d. are even more complex, consisting of one or more atoms held together by bonds.

52.

Element	Classification
Nickel (Ni)	Metal
Xenon (Xe)	Noble Gas
Radon (Rn)	Noble Gas
Neon (Ne)	Noble Gas
Silicon (Si)	Nonmetal

Nickel is a metal. Xenon, radon, and neon are noble gasses. They are also nonmetals, but they are more specifically noble gasses. Silicon is a nonmetal, but it is not a noble gas.

How to Overcome Test Anxiety

Just the thought of taking a test is enough to make most people a little nervous. A test is an important event that can have a long-term impact on your future, so it's important to take it seriously and it's natural to feel anxious about performing well. But just because anxiety is normal, that doesn't mean that it's helpful in test taking, or that you should simply accept it as part of your life. Anxiety can have a variety of effects. These effects can be mild, like making you feel slightly nervous, or severe, like blocking your ability to focus or remember even a simple detail.

If you experience test anxiety—whether severe or mild—it's important to know how to beat it. To discover this, first you need to understand what causes test anxiety.

Causes of Test Anxiety

While we often think of anxiety as an uncontrollable emotional state, it can actually be caused by simple, practical things. One of the most common causes of test anxiety is that a person does not feel adequately prepared for their test. This feeling can be the result of many different issues such as poor study habits or lack of organization, but the most common culprit is time management. Starting to study too late, failing to organize your study time to cover all of the material, or being distracted while you study will mean that you're not well prepared for the test. This may lead to cramming the night before, which will cause you to be physically and mentally exhausted for the test. Poor time management also contributes to feelings of stress, fear, and hopelessness as you realize you are not well prepared but don't know what to do about it.

Other times, test anxiety is not related to your preparation for the test but comes from unresolved fear. This may be a past failure on a test, or poor performance on tests in general. It may come from comparing yourself to others who seem to be performing better or from the stress of living up to expectations. Anxiety may be driven by fears of the future—how failure on this test would affect your educational and career goals. These fears are often completely irrational, but they can still negatively impact your test performance.

Elements of Test Anxiety

As mentioned earlier, test anxiety is considered to be an emotional state, but it has physical and mental components as well. Sometimes you may not even realize that you are suffering from test anxiety until you notice the physical symptoms. These can include trembling hands, rapid heartbeat, sweating, nausea, and tense muscles. Extreme anxiety may lead to fainting or vomiting. Obviously, any of these symptoms can have a negative impact on testing. It is important to recognize them as soon as they begin to occur so that you can address the problem before it damages your performance.

The mental components of test anxiety include trouble focusing and inability to remember learned information. During a test, your mind is on high alert, which can help you recall information and stay focused for an extended period of time. However, anxiety interferes with your mind's natural processes, causing you to blank out, even on the questions you know well. The strain of testing during anxiety makes it difficult to stay focused, especially on a test that may take several hours. Extreme anxiety can take a huge mental toll, making it difficult not only to recall test information but even to understand the test questions or pull your thoughts together.

Effects of Test Anxiety

Test anxiety is like a disease—if left untreated, it will get progressively worse. Anxiety leads to poor performance, and this reinforces the feelings of fear and failure, which in turn lead to poor performances on subsequent tests. It can grow from a mild nervousness to a crippling condition. If allowed to progress, test anxiety can have a big impact on your schooling, and consequently on your future.

Test anxiety can spread to other parts of your life. Anxiety on tests can become anxiety in any stressful situation, and blanking on a test can turn into panicking in a job situation. But fortunately, you don't have to let anxiety rule your testing and determine your grades. There are a number of relatively simple steps you can take to move past anxiety and function normally on a test and in the rest of life.

Physical Steps for Beating Test Anxiety

While test anxiety is a serious problem, the good news is that it can be overcome. It doesn't have to control your ability to think and remember information. While it may take time, you can begin taking steps today to beat anxiety.

Just as your first hint that you may be struggling with anxiety comes from the physical symptoms, the first step to treating it is also physical. Rest is crucial for having a clear, strong mind. If you are tired, it is much easier to give in to anxiety. But if you establish good sleep habits, your body and mind will be ready to perform optimally, without the strain of exhaustion. Additionally, sleeping well helps you to retain information better, so you're more likely to recall the answers when you see the test questions.

Getting good sleep means more than going to bed on time. It's important to allow your brain time to relax. Take study breaks from time to time so it doesn't get overworked, and don't study right before bed. Take time to rest your mind before trying to rest your body, or you may find it difficult to fall asleep.

Along with sleep, other aspects of physical health are important in preparing for a test. Good nutrition is vital for good brain function. Sugary foods and drinks may give a burst of energy but this burst is followed by a crash, both physically and emotionally. Instead, fuel your body with protein and vitamin-rich foods.

Also, drink plenty of water. Dehydration can lead to headaches and exhaustion, especially if your brain is already under stress from the rigors of the test. Particularly if your test is a long one, drink water during the breaks. And if possible, take an energy-boosting snack to eat between sections.

Along with sleep and diet, a third important part of physical health is exercise. Maintaining a steady workout schedule is helpful, but even taking 5-minute study breaks to walk can help get your blood pumping faster and clear your head. Exercise also releases endorphins, which contribute to a positive feeling and can help combat test anxiety.

When you nurture your physical health, you are also contributing to your mental health. If your body is healthy, your mind is much more likely to be healthy as well. So take time to rest, nourish your body with healthy food and water, and get moving as much as possible. Taking these physical steps will make you stronger and more able to take the mental steps necessary to overcome test anxiety.

Mental Steps for Beating Test Anxiety

Working on the mental side of test anxiety can be more challenging, but as with the physical side, there are clear steps you can take to overcome it. As mentioned earlier, test anxiety often stems from lack of preparation, so the obvious solution is to prepare for the test. Effective studying may be the most important weapon you have for beating test anxiety, but you can and should employ several other mental tools to combat fear.

First, boost your confidence by reminding yourself of past success—tests or projects that you aced. If you're putting as much effort into preparing for this test as you did for those, there's no reason you should expect to fail here. Work hard to prepare; then trust your preparation.

Second, surround yourself with encouraging people. It can be helpful to find a study group, but be sure that the people you're around will encourage a positive attitude. If you spend time with others who are anxious or cynical, this will only contribute to your own anxiety. Look for others who are motivated to study hard from a desire to succeed, not from a fear of failure.

Third, reward yourself. A test is physically and mentally tiring, even without anxiety, and it can be helpful to have something to look forward to. Plan an activity following the test, regardless of the outcome, such as going to a movie or getting ice cream.

When you are taking the test, if you find yourself beginning to feel anxious, remind yourself that you know the material. Visualize successfully completing the test. Then take a few deep, relaxing breaths and return to it. Work through the questions carefully but with confidence, knowing that you are capable of succeeding.

Developing a healthy mental approach to test taking will also aid in other areas of life. Test anxiety affects more than just the actual test—it can be damaging to your mental health and even contribute to depression. It's important to beat test anxiety before it becomes a problem for more than testing.

Study Strategy

Being prepared for the test is necessary to combat anxiety, but what does being prepared look like? You may study for hours on end and still not feel prepared. What you need is a strategy for test prep. The next few pages outline our recommended steps to help you plan out and conquer the challenge of preparation.

Step 1: Scope Out the Test

Learn everything you can about the format (multiple choice, essay, etc.) and what will be on the test. Gather any study materials, course outlines, or sample exams that may be available. Not only will this help you to prepare, but knowing what to expect can help to alleviate test anxiety.

Step 2: Map Out the Material

Look through the textbook or study guide and make note of how many chapters or sections it has. Then divide these over the time you have. For example, if a book has 15 chapters and you have five days to study, you need to cover three chapters each day. Even better, if you have the time, leave an extra day at the end for overall review after you have gone through the material in depth.

If time is limited, you may need to prioritize the material. Look through it and make note of which sections you think you already have a good grasp on, and which need review. While you are studying, skim quickly through the familiar sections and take more time on the challenging parts.

Write out your plan so you don't get lost as you go. Having a written plan also helps you feel more in control of the study, so anxiety is less likely to arise from feeling overwhelmed at the amount to cover.

Step 3: Gather Your Tools

Decide what study method works best for you. Do you prefer to highlight in the book as you study and then go back over the highlighted portions? Or do you type out notes of the important information? Or is it helpful to make flashcards that you can carry with you? Assemble the pens, index cards, highlighters, post-it notes, and any other materials you may need so you won't be distracted by getting up to find things while you study.

If you're having a hard time retaining the information or organizing your notes, experiment with different methods. For example, try color-coding by subject with colored pens, highlighters, or post-it notes. If you learn better by hearing, try recording yourself reading your notes so you can listen while in the car, working out, or simply sitting at your desk. Ask a friend to quiz you from your flashcards, or try teaching someone the material to solidify it in your mind.

Step 4: Create Your Environment

It's important to avoid distractions while you study. This includes both the obvious distractions like visitors and the subtle distractions like an uncomfortable chair (or a too-comfortable couch that makes you want to fall asleep). Set up the best study environment possible: good lighting and a comfortable work area. If background music helps you focus, you may want to turn it on, but otherwise keep the room quiet. If you are using a computer to take notes, be sure you don't have any other windows open, especially applications like social media, games, or anything else that could distract you. Silence your phone and turn off notifications. Be sure to keep water close by so you stay hydrated while you study (but avoid unhealthy drinks and snacks).

Also, take into account the best time of day to study. Are you freshest first thing in the morning? Try to set aside some time then to work through the material. Is your mind clearer in the afternoon or evening? Schedule your study session then. Another method is to study at the same time of day that you will take the test, so that your brain gets used to working on the material at that time and will be ready to focus at test time.

Step 5: Study!

Once you have done all the study preparation, it's time to settle into the actual studying. Sit down, take a few moments to settle your mind so you can focus, and begin to follow your study plan. Don't give in to distractions or let yourself procrastinate. This is your time to prepare so you'll be ready to fearlessly approach the test. Make the most of the time and stay focused.

Of course, you don't want to burn out. If you study too long you may find that you're not retaining the information very well. Take regular study breaks. For example, taking five minutes out of every hour to walk briskly, breathing deeply and swinging your arms, can help your mind stay fresh.

As you get to the end of each chapter or section, it's a good idea to do a quick review. Remind yourself of what you learned and work on any difficult parts. When you feel that you've mastered the material, move on to the next part. At the end of your study session, briefly skim through your notes again.

But while review is helpful, cramming last minute is NOT. If at all possible, work ahead so that you won't need to fit all your study into the last day. Cramming overloads your brain with more information than it can process and retain, and your tired mind may struggle to recall even previously learned information when it is overwhelmed with last-minute study. Also, the urgent nature of cramming and the stress placed on your brain contribute to anxiety. You'll be more likely to go to the test feeling unprepared and having trouble thinking clearly.

So don't cram, and don't stay up late before the test, even just to review your notes at a leisurely pace. Your brain needs rest more than it needs to go over the information again. In fact, plan to finish your studies by noon or early afternoon the day before the test. Give your brain the rest of the day to relax or focus on other things, and get a good night's sleep. Then you will be fresh for the test and better able to recall what you've studied.

Step 6: Take a Practice Test

Many courses offer sample tests, either online or in the study materials. This is an excellent resource to check whether you have mastered the material, as well as to prepare for the test format and environment.

Check the test format ahead of time: the number of questions, the type (multiple choice, free response, etc.), and the time limit. Then create a plan for working through them. For example, if you have 30 minutes to take a 60-question test, your limit is 30 seconds per question. Spend less time on the questions you know well so that you can take more time on the difficult ones.

If you have time to take several practice tests, take the first one open book, with no time limit. Work through the questions at your own pace and make sure you fully understand them. Gradually work up to taking a test under test conditions: sit at a desk with all study materials put away and set a timer. Pace yourself to make sure you finish the test with time to spare and go back to check your answers if you have time.

After each test, check your answers. On the questions you missed, be sure you understand why you missed them. Did you misread the question (tests can use tricky wording)? Did you forget the information? Or was it something you hadn't learned? Go back and study any shaky areas that the practice tests reveal.

Taking these tests not only helps with your grade, but also aids in combating test anxiety. If you're already used to the test conditions, you're less likely to worry about it, and working through tests until you're scoring well gives you a confidence boost. Go through the practice tests until you feel comfortable, and then you can go into the test knowing that you're ready for it.

Test Tips

On test day, you should be confident, knowing that you've prepared well and are ready to answer the questions. But aside from preparation, there are several test day strategies you can employ to maximize your performance.

First, as stated before, get a good night's sleep the night before the test (and for several nights before that, if possible). Go into the test with a fresh, alert mind rather than staying up late to study.

Try not to change too much about your normal routine on the day of the test. It's important to eat a nutritious breakfast, but if you normally don't eat breakfast at all, consider eating just a protein bar. If you're a coffee drinker, go ahead and have your normal coffee. Just make sure you time it so that the caffeine doesn't wear off right in the middle of your test. Avoid sugary beverages, and drink enough water to stay hydrated but not so much that you need a restroom break 10 minutes into the test. If your test isn't first thing in the morning, consider going for a walk or doing a light workout before the test to get your blood flowing.

Allow yourself enough time to get ready, and leave for the test with plenty of time to spare so you won't have the anxiety of scrambling to arrive in time. Another reason to be early is to select a good seat. It's helpful to sit away from doors and windows, which can be distracting. Find a good seat, get out your supplies, and settle your mind before the test begins.

When the test begins, start by going over the instructions carefully, even if you already know what to expect. Make sure you avoid any careless mistakes by following the directions.

Then begin working through the questions, pacing yourself as you've practiced. If you're not sure on an answer, don't spend too much time on it, and don't let it shake your confidence. Either skip it and come back later, or eliminate as many wrong answers as possible and guess among the remaining ones. Don't dwell on these questions as you continue—put them out of your mind and focus on what lies ahead.

Be sure to read all of the answer choices, even if you're sure the first one is the right answer. Sometimes you'll find a better one if you keep reading. But don't second-guess yourself if you do immediately know the answer. Your gut instinct is usually right. Don't let test anxiety rob you of the information you know.

If you have time at the end of the test (and if the test format allows), go back and review your answers. Be cautious about changing any, since your first instinct tends to be correct, but make sure you didn't misread any of the questions or accidentally mark the wrong answer choice. Look over any you skipped and make an educated guess.

At the end, leave the test feeling confident. You've done your best, so don't waste time worrying about your performance or wishing you could change anything. Instead, celebrate the successful completion of this test. And finally, use this test to learn how to deal with anxiety even better next time.

Review Video: Test Anxiety
Visit mometrix.com/academy and enter code: 100340

Important Qualification

Not all anxiety is created equal. If your test anxiety is causing major issues in your life beyond the classroom or testing center, or if you are experiencing troubling physical symptoms related to your anxiety, it may be a sign of a serious physiological or psychological condition. If this sounds like your situation, we strongly encourage you to seek professional help.

Online Resources

Due to our efforts to try to keep this book to a manageable length, we've created a link that will give you access to all of your online resources:

mometrix.com/resources719/ssncg8sci

It's Your Moment, Let's Celebrate It!

Share your story @mometrixtestpreparation